CULTIVATE
THE PROCESS OF LIVING FROM YOUR HEART

cultivate
cul·ti·vate \ˈkəl-tə-ˌvāt\

: to prepare and use for the raising of crops
: to loosen or break up the soil
: to foster the growth of
: to improve by labor, care or study
: further, encourage
: to seek the society of
: make friends with

WELCOME

A NOTE TO THE READER

One of the greatest things our community cultivates is relationship with the Holy Spirit in every part of life. The writings in this book were inspired by moments when we encountered the Lord in the middle of our ordinary, mundane tasks and schedules. We make beautiful discoveries when we dare to believe He desires to speak through these simple moments of everyday life.

In these pages you will find recipes for spending time with the Lord and be prompted to journal His voice. Jesus says in John 10:27, "My sheep hear my voice, and I know them, and they follow me" (ESV). As a child of God, you know His voice; you hear Him, and it is important that you record, savor and declare His thoughts over your life. By recording His thoughts, you will remember how deeply He loves you and who you truly are. Be courageous! It is in this process that our minds are transformed and we are able to live confidently as His sons and daughters.

We encourage you to center your heart in this simple truth: God is a loving Father, ready and eager to speak to you. It is our hope that through these pages, you will be inspired to draw close to Him, that you will come into a better understanding of His nature and that you will dare to believe that you are who He says you are.

01

LAYING THE FOUNDATION

*foundation*₂ : the lowest load-bearing part of a building,
             typically below ground level.
        : an underlying basis or principle for something.

10	FLY HIGH BUILD HOME
15	WHO DO YOU SAY I AM?
16	ALL MY OWN
18	BLUEBIRDS
21	THE COTTAGE
22	ACCESS TO WATER
25	CRANES
27	BLANKET OF TRUST
28	SATURATED IN KINDNESS
31	THE FATHER'S SONG
35	PATIENCE IN THE MESS
36	SOFT CLAY
39	ROOTBOUND
40	IN THE EARLY HOURS
41	IN THE EVENING

02

BEGIN THE ASCENT

ascend₃ : go up or climb to the summit of a mountain or hill.
: rise through the air.

45	SEASONING YOUR CAST IRON SKILLET
49	SYMPATHY VS. EMPATHY
51	FEEDING THE FIVE THOUSAND
52	TYING LOOSE ENDS
53	LIVING FROM BLESSING
55	STEWARDING GOD'S GIFTS
56	THE BALANCE
58	MACARONS
59	POPPYSEED TO LEMON
63	WHO TENDS THE FOREST?
65	FROM THE GARDEN
71	DELIVERY CONFIRMATION

03
HARNESS THE WIND

soaring~4~ : maintain height in the air without flapping wings or using engine power.
: fly or rise high in the air.

74	SOMETIMES THE SKY IS TOO BRIGHT
77	SOARING IN REMEMBRANCE
79	MARTHA'S TABLE
82	FROM THE AIRPLANE WINDOW ON A CLOUDLESS NIGHT
84	FREEDOM THROUGH TRUST
85	PERSPECTIVE
86	SUSPENDED IN SAFETY
87	SONG OF REDEMPTION
88	MOTIVATED TO LOVE HIM
89	SOARING IN THE WORKPLACE
90	PERMISSION

04

EMBRACE THE RETURN

landing$_5$: an instance of coming or bringing something to
land, either from the air or from water.

94	LANDING
95	GRANDFATHER'S HANDS
97	A MIGRATION OF WHALES
100	WONDER
102	SLOWING DOWN
108	CANCEL THE DISTANCE
109	CHILDLIKENESS
111	MY YOUNG QUEEN
113	PRAYER
115	AFTERMATH

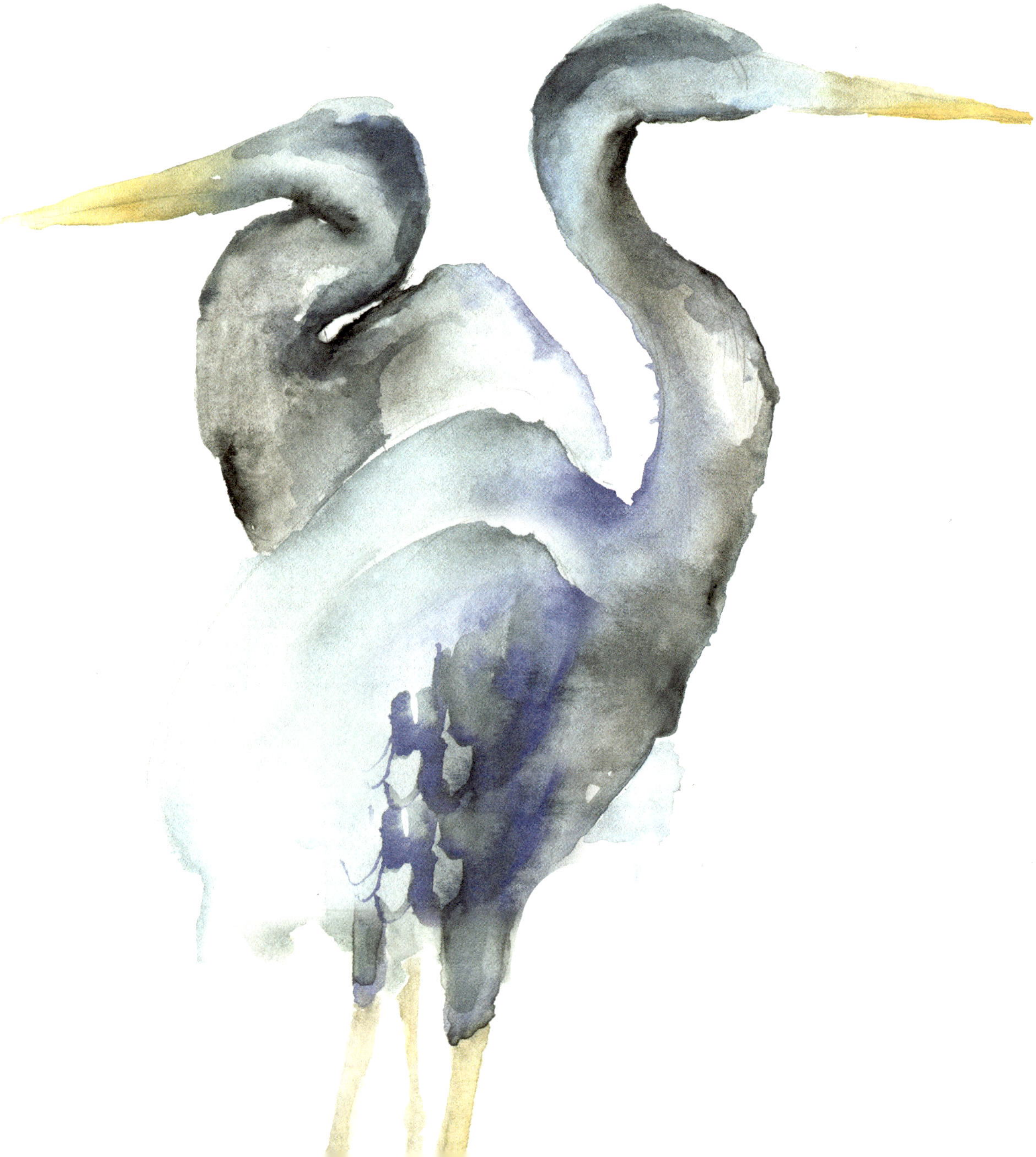

laying the foundation

"...YOU ARE GOD'S HOUSE. USING THE GIFT GOD GAVE ME AS A GOOD ARCHITECT, I DESIGNED BLUEPRINTS; APOLLOS IS PUTTING UP THE WALLS. LET EACH CARPENTER WHO COMES ON THE JOB TAKE CARE TO BUILD ON THE FOUNDATION! REMEMBER, THERE IS ONLY ONE FOUNDATION, THE ONE ALREADY LAID: JESUS CHRIST."

1 CORINTHIANS 3:10-11, MSG

FLY HIGH BUILD HOME

OPENING THOUGHTS BY MELISSA HELSER
ILLUSTRATION BY JUSTINA STEVENS

Those defining moments in life. The Father speaks and it resounds in our internal worlds. One sentence from His mouth suddenly alters the direction of our lives, it plants vision and sustains us forever. Those simple but profound occasions linger throughout our lifetime. We unpack their simplicities when we are young—unravel their complexities when we're old.

Fly High, Build Home—I think I will be unpacking this one for a long time, perhaps my whole life...

Our community was about to launch the Cageless Birds and wanted a clear mission statement to help communicate our values. We had grown so much in the last eight years. Jonathan and I wanted to launch something that was beyond us, something that would be a catalyst for our whole community. Creating a mission statement isn't easy. A true and clear mission statement isn't just what you want to become, but what you already are. We were in a staff meeting talking through our values, listing out all of the things we believe. I remember the moment I said, "We fly high, but we build home." It came out of my mouth and swirled around all of us in the room. It was more than a mission statement, it was what we were in the moment and what we are becoming. Since then we have been discovering its truth in our everyday lives. We have only begun to scratch the surface, and the more we dig into this simple saying, the more we are undone by the limitless layers of its truth. It has challenged our community to ask the Father questions. It has pressed us to seek out His voice in a fresh way.

We live in a culture that puts extreme importance on flying high, and yet little value on what consumes the majority of our lives: home. If our flying high moments are not rooted in home, they can become a tireless journey of reaching for unattainable goals, figuring out our calling in our own strength, asking ourselves over and over, *What am I here for?* It is so important to learn to build home in the inner chambers of our hearts. It is the place we plant and watch love, patience, kindness, gentleness, joy, peace, goodness, faithfulness and self-control grow into an orchard. The fruit of this orchard is eternal; it not only will satisfy you, but will create a legacy of the nature of the Lord. You see, the fruit of the Spirit is not something you reach out and grab when you need it; it is something that grows from a life planted in the nature of God. This fruit matures us into whole people who fully enjoy life. This is the home we want to build.

I want to provoke a generation to give their lives to building a home with the Father, Son and Spirit. Jesus told us to pray, "On Earth as it is in Heaven." On Earth, in my world, in my everyday, just like it is in Heaven. Whether you are single or married, a teenager or a mature adult, whether you are a child or an elderly person, pray that your life would look like Heaven's culture. What an incredible thing that Jesus instructed us to pray like that! He desired for us to be empowered with the understanding that He wants to come even more than we want Him to. We don't just have to hold on by a thread to this life and wait to get to Heaven—we get to love this life we have been given and create an atmosphere of Heaven wherever we are. When we believe that truth it changes everything.

I want to suggest that home as a posture of understanding is more valuable to your life than home as a house or residence.

Jesus created home everywhere.

I believe that Jesus lingered in humanity, thirty years unspoken for, so that He could truly fall in love with what He was going to die for. He spent thirty years of His life on Earth doing the glorious every day. He tithed a tenth of His life on Earth to ministry, and when He did ministry, it looked like family. It looked like home. It looked like meals and laughter, tears and sorrow, walking and talking and intentionally living life together. It looked liked flying-high moments of feeding the five thousand, healing the crowds, speaking on the mountain to the hungry hearts, seeing eyesight returned and endless bleeding stop, and then effortlessly landing emotionally, spiritually and physically with a tiny group of friends. He knew how to teach them to fly high in faith and boldness and then to land in a home of friendship with each other and understanding of the Kingdom.

We must be careful not to over-spiritualize the life of Jesus. It is sacred and holy, but Jesus clothed Himself in our human skin so that we could feel seen and loved in the shell that sometimes feels so restricting. When we know that Jesus loves our humanity, we are able to embrace it in a clear and more effortless way. We are able to savor the moments that feel insignificant and build an eternal home there.

I have learned that I am actually the truest version of myself when I am surrounded by those who know me the deepest. I breathe deep and give in to the simplicity of being known. I love standing on a stage and leading thousands into the throne room, the moments of speaking and feeling the beauty of the Holy Spirit swirling around me. I love the moments where I feel like I am fulfilling the grand question, *"What is my calling?"* If I am honest, in my youth I craved applause for a job well done to fill my inner world. But as I get older, I am learning to pay attention to what I am really feeling: Are those moments really sustaining me?

My moments of glory are changing. Like the moment around a table when our community finishes a school and we are feasting in the natural and in the Spirit, recollecting all that the Lord did. It isn't just that He used me but that He used all of us, everyone in the family carried the weight, and we all feel the reward. I listen to all the moments I wasn't there for. I remember that the sacrifice of laying down my life for another human is always worth it. I sit in those moments and cry. They are the moments that build a foundation in my heart that is unshakeable. These are the foundations that have THE GOSPEL OF JESUS written on them. These moments around the table are as significant as every grand moment we are celebrating. We are all in love with the Gospel more than we ever were, and we realize that without Him everything is impossible. When we allow our hearts to get caught up in gratitude, thanksgiving strengthens our foundations. And then the moment that I thought I was building home has turned into a flying high moment.

I am here to tell you that my version of flying high has changed dramatically over my life. I build home and feel the sensation of flying high every day I wake up and choose kindness and grace, when I choose mercy and release true forgiveness. I am flying high in moments where no one sees me. These are the times I feel like I am soaring high in the sky with no flapping at all, the times where I effortlessly, subconsciously choose love. I am learning to look back on those moments and smile and see that the growth I crave is actually happening. The orchard is growing.

"Fly High, Build Home" has become the track that keeps us centered and stable. It is the beauty of the simple and the grand. The longer we live by it, the more blurred the lines get. The times I think I am flying high, I am actually building home, and the times I think I am building home, I am actually flying high. It is all becoming the same and different and deeply significant.

We are not trying to eloquently explain our mission statement. We are too young to try to sum up the goal of our lives. We are but pilgrims on a journey to discover a truer, more beautiful life rooted in slowing down and savoring that which is really important. We don't want to get to the end of our lives and wish we had really taken it all in. Oh that we would listen stronger and speak more confidently and live a life worthy of celebration. We are reaching far beyond our capacity. Desiring to live a life of dreaming and seeing our dreams become reality. We are not stagnant in our pursuit of excellence. We dream and plan and produce, just like the parable of the talents. When our Master comes, He will look us in the eyes and say, "Well done, you multiplied what I gave you." Let us embrace the tension. It is not one or the other, but both. In the great tension, our lives create a symphony of rises and falls. The selahs are as important as the crescendos. They all have a place.

Our prayer is that this issue would inspire you to reach and root and not be afraid of the pressing in or the silence. That you would experience the joy of seeing beyond your capacity, opening your wings and feeling the free air calling you higher. May you feel the effortless moments of soaring high and the joy of landing.

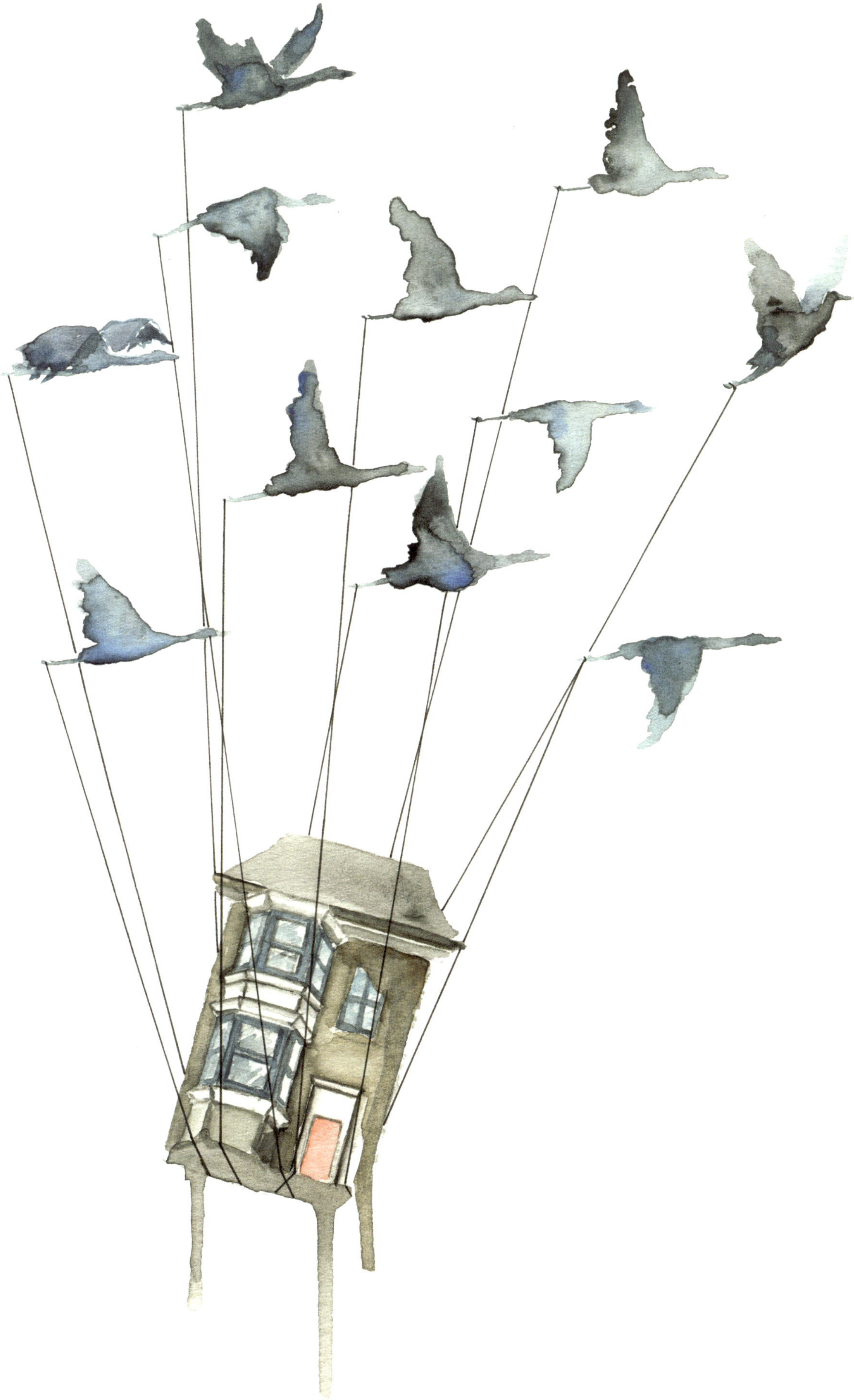

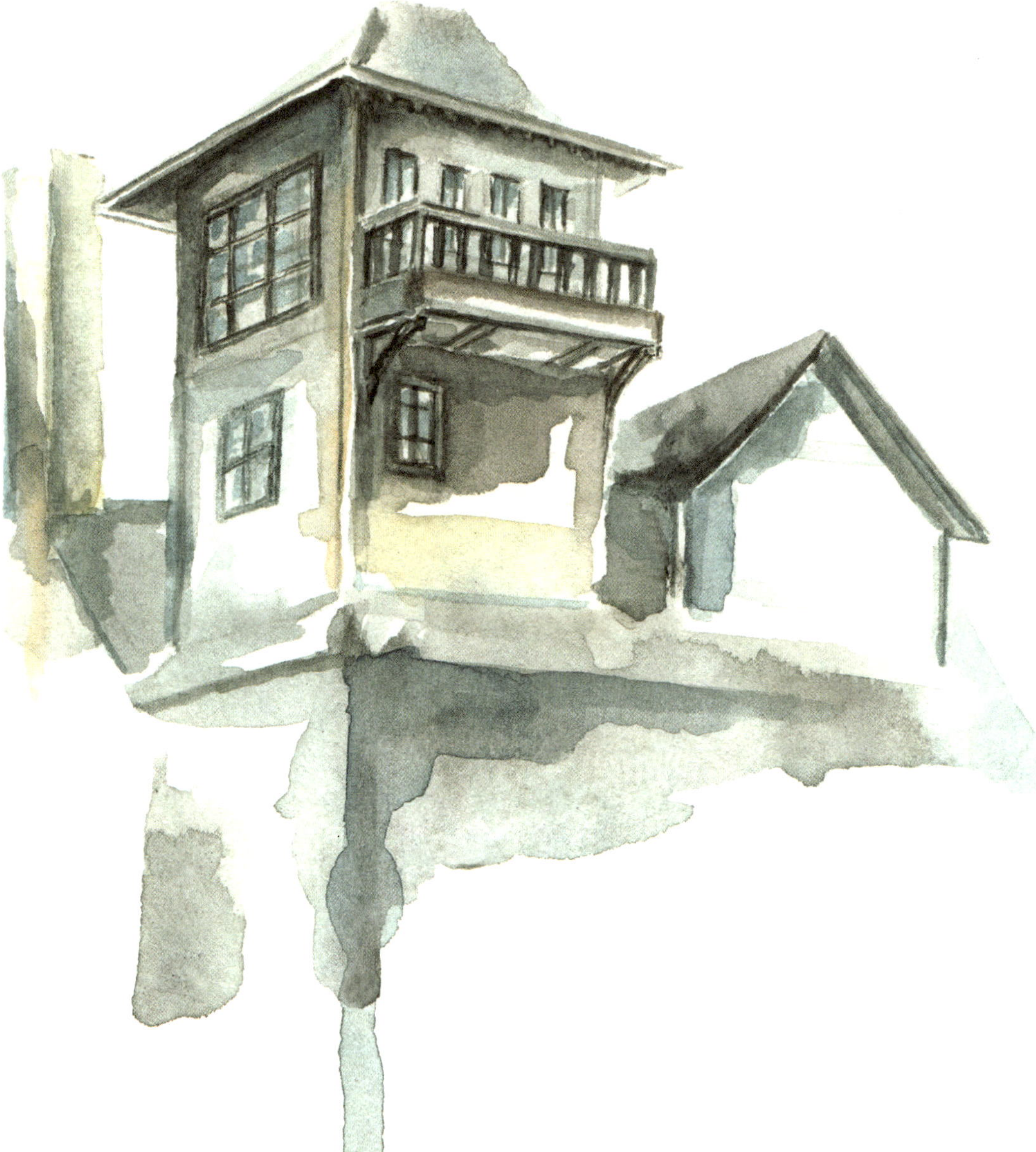

NO. 1

WHO DO YOU SAY I AM?

RECIPE FOR IDENTITY / BY JONATHAN DAVID HELSER / PAINTING BY JUSTINA STEVENS

I will never forget a moment I had with my wife when we were falling head-over-heels in love. We were out on a magical date night at a sensational restaurant, seated at a cozy table. At one point during our meal, we found ourselves so smitten with love that we stopped eating and just sat there, gazing deep into each other's eyes. I am sure we looked absolutely foolish, but that's what love can make you do. As we were looking at one another, I saw my reflection in her eyes. The eyes of the one I was falling in love with became a mirror for me to see myself. It was one of those defining instances when your heart is marked with something eternal.

A few years after that date night, I had another face-to-face moment when my son was born. As I held him for the first time, he opened his eyes, and it happened again. I saw myself staring back at me in the eyes of someone I was falling deeply in love with. In my son's eyes, I saw myself. I began to think about that first encounter Adam had with God in the garden, when God held him face-to-face and kissed him with life. Life began there; Adam opened his eyes for the first time and saw the face of God. In those eyes of pure love, Adam saw who he was. The eyes of God became the mirror that defined Adam.

Take a moment, and read the story of Jesus asking His disciples who He is in Matthew 16:13-20.

What an incredible face-to-face moment Jesus had with Peter. "Who do you say I am?" Did Jesus ask this question because He had forgotten who He was, or because He wanted Peter to truly see who He was? As Peter stops to see who Jesus really is, he exclaims, "You are the Christ the Son of the Living God...." Then Jesus introduces Peter to his identity: "You are Peter and on this Rock I will build my church." In this interchange, Peter sees the Christ and then discovers who He is. Jesus becomes the mirror of Peter's true identity. Jesus restores the keys and the authority that were given away in the garden.

Prompt: Psalm 23 says that the Lord leads us to still waters to restore our soul. In still waters you can see your reflection. When we stop and remember who God is, we discover who we are, and we are restored to our original identity. Get two pieces of paper or use two blank pages in your journal. Write this question at the top of each page: Who do you say I am? On the first page, this is the question God is asking you. So take your pen and write down who God is to you. On the second page, ask God the same question. By faith, listen to His voice and His love. Now begin to write who He says you are. When you finish writing, declare it out loud!

NO. 2

ALL MY OWN

RECIPE FOR OWNERSHIP / BY ERIN GRAVITT / PHOTO BY SYDNEE MELA

During my high-speed college years, I insisted upon filling up my days and nights with something to do: events, functions, parties, volunteerism, meetings. The goal was always to get out of the house and do something "cool" and "worthwhile" with my time and friends. Staying at home with nothing to do seemed like such a waste. I came home solely to sleep. My mother used to admonish me, "You've got to learn the value of staying at home. One day you will realize how good home is." I remember shaking my head at her while I rushed out the door with my car keys in hand, heaving a sigh, "She doesn't get it."

Fast-forward to present-day newlywed life. After foregoing an out-of-town concert at the last minute with the excuse, "We don't feel like it," my husband looked at me and asked cautiously, "Are we homebodies?" I heaved another sigh, but this one of defeat. Ten years down the road, and my rush had worn me down. I discovered that I had indeed become a homebody and that my mother was right. I never thought that staying would become more enjoyable than going, but it had. And to my surprise, it was a good thing!

The quaint home I now share with my husband and six-month-old daughter is safe, warm and familiar. Photos of family and loved ones illuminate every corner; they breathe happy memories of our journey. There is a fridge that's fully stocked and a pantry of groceries bought with our hard-earned money—and always a dozen eggs for the husband who loves breakfast omelettes. Each room holds furniture that can tell stories, all generously given by our loved ones and community after our wedding and when our daughter was born. I love this place and my slower pace in this season. My home is all my own.

Ownership has made all the difference. When home finally became something that I built and put my own blood, sweat, tears and money into, I came to genuinely value it. When my hard work and prayer poured into a place that was all mine, it made me long to stay and take advantage of it. Responsibility gave me motivation to clean, maintain and beautify. Being a homebody became a desirable title when it held hands with ownership.

Prompt: As children of God, the way we take care and manage the gifts God gives us is important. "For where your treasure is, there your heart will be also" (Matthew 6:21, NIV). Perhaps you don't own or rent a home, but consider for a moment something that belongs to you. What do you own and take care of? Ask the Lord how you can be a proper steward of that gift, however great or small. The responsibility, joy and reward can be yours. Also ask Him, "Lord is there a gift that someone has given me that I've neglected to take care of? Forgive me. Show me how I can take ownership of that gift and bless you and others by stewarding it well."

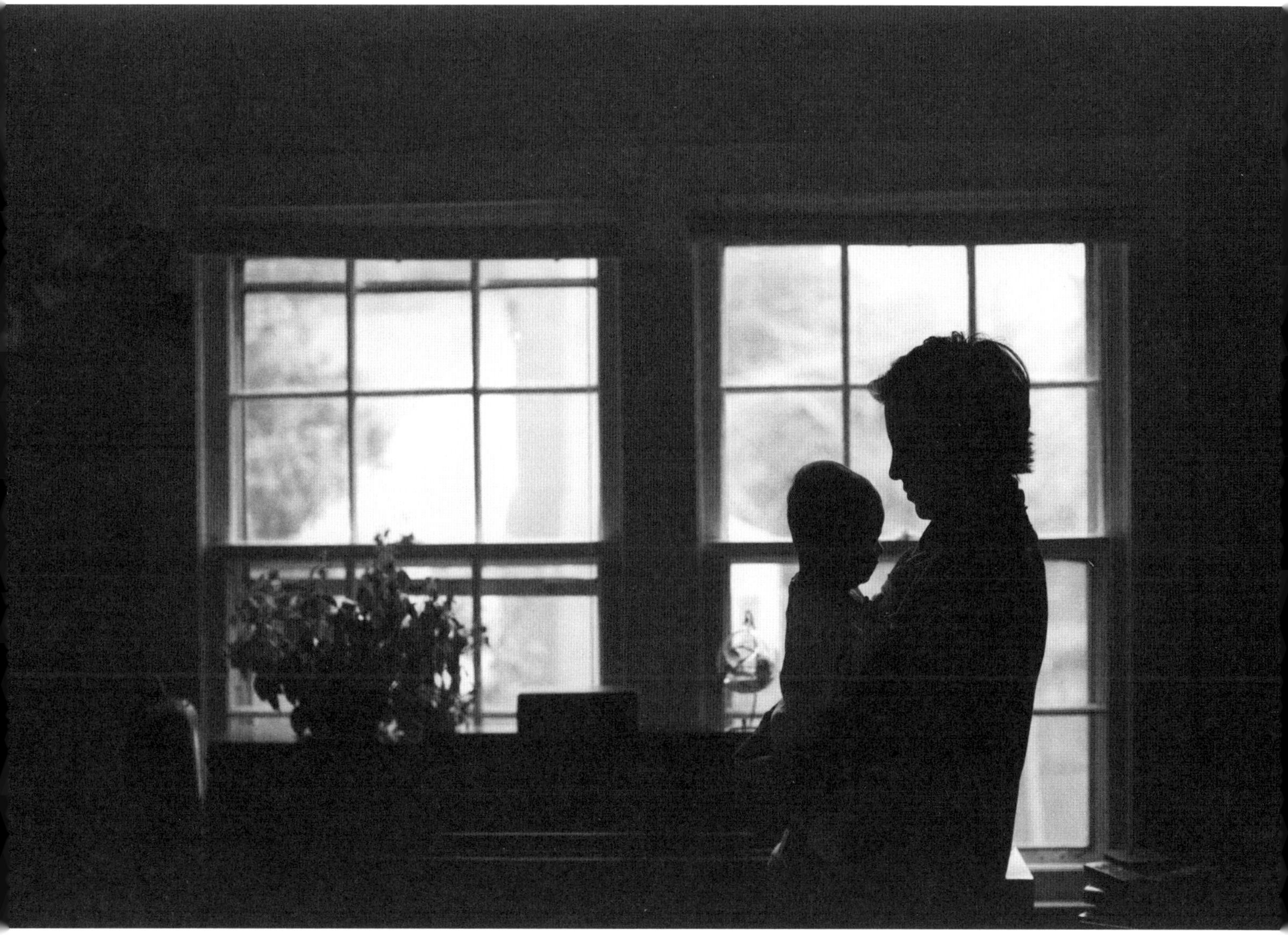

NO. 3

BLUEBIRDS

RECIPE FOR PERSEVERANCE / WRITING AND PAINTING BY KEN HELSER

Few of God's creatures evoke as much emotion in song as the little bluebird. The saga of the bluebird is a dramatic story of its struggle for survival and its ability to defy extinction.

Why did these little birds that carry the sky on their wings have to fight to stay around? Because of its many enemies. First, it was the environment. Highways, super malls and housing projects rapidly eroded the wild berry trees that once sustained the bird in the winter. The hollows in trees and fence posts which once served as bluebird homes were destroyed. Then came the raccoons and black snakes that invade the home of the bluebird for an easy meal; the starlings, robbing its food supply; and the English sparrow, that savagely kills the mother and robs the nest. Some wondered if the bluebird could possibly survive, and some decided to give God's little creature a hand.

These little birds are thriving thanks to Jack Finch, a Carolinian who built more than 50,000 bluebird boxes, and planted the berry producing dogwoods for the bluebird's winter provisions with more vigor than Johnny Appleseed planted apple trees. Mr. Finch first caught my attention when he was featured on an Earth Day special on CBS News. I was instantly captivated by the Jesus look in his eye. When asked why he would spend much of his life building homes for bluebirds, he remarked, "Well, one day this old body will be laid to rest, and I'd like to think a bluebird or two might take notice of my love for them and sing a song or two over my grave." I was so intrigued by the nurseryman from Bailey, North Carolina, that Linda and I sought him out in hopes of taking some photos of the beautiful birds which I hoped to make a painting of. But we got much more. We got a life-changing message.

"Did you know that bluebirds are very romantic?" Mr. Finch said, tilting his ear to catch the warble of a songbird in the distance. "Yep. The male bird falls in love and courts his sweetheart by first finding a suitable home for them to nest. From there he sings his love song. That's what attracts her. If she says 'I do' to his proposal by entering the future homesite, he flutters wildly and sings his head off with joy! It's a site to behold."

"Why, that's just like Jesus!" I exclaimed, reveling in the correlation between the bird and the Gospel. "Christ has gone to prepare a place for us, and from there He attracts us, His bride-to-be, to His house with His own love song!"

I was plumb giddy from the revelation, when the kind man continued, "And bluebirds are not only romantic, they are faithful to each other. They mate for life. They make such great parents that they are one of the few birds in existence that continue to feed their young after they leave the nest. Why, they even take a family vacation," he laughed. "They migrate south as a family."

I could see that Jack was choking with emotion. Not for the birds, but for mankind. Turning away to hide the tear in his eye, he spoke solemnly, "There is so much we could learn from God's little creatures if we would only pay attention. The bluebird is such an overcomer. They have so many enemies. So many obstacles to overcome. But they never seem to waste their lives by complaining. They just energetically go on building their homes, their families, with hope. A great big hope that it's all going to work out fine…"

After visiting many bluebird houses around Jack's farm, and taking hundreds of pictures, the kind man loaded five bird boxes into our van and gave us a hug that implied we had become friends for life.

As we drove out on the long dirt road from Jack's place, we passed one bluebird box after another. I found myself saluting every homesite—every House of Hope. I think I was subconsciously saying thank you to God's little creatures who taught me about overcoming. Conquering fear. Romance and faithfulness. And victory. I too wanted to go home and build my own House of Hope.

"'I know the plans I have for you,' declares the Lord, 'plans to prosper you and not to harm you, plans to give you hope and a future'" (Jeremiah 29:11, NIV).

Prompt: Go outside and find a place to sit. Bring your journal and pen with you. Let yourself sit in the quiet for a while and ask yourself, "Am I complaining in the middle of my struggle, or energetically going on building home?" If you find that you are in a tough spot and complaining is normal, journal this question to the Father, "God, what does energetically going on building home look like for me in this time of my life?" Journal His response.

This is one of my favorite cards! Remember who you are —
— Jana

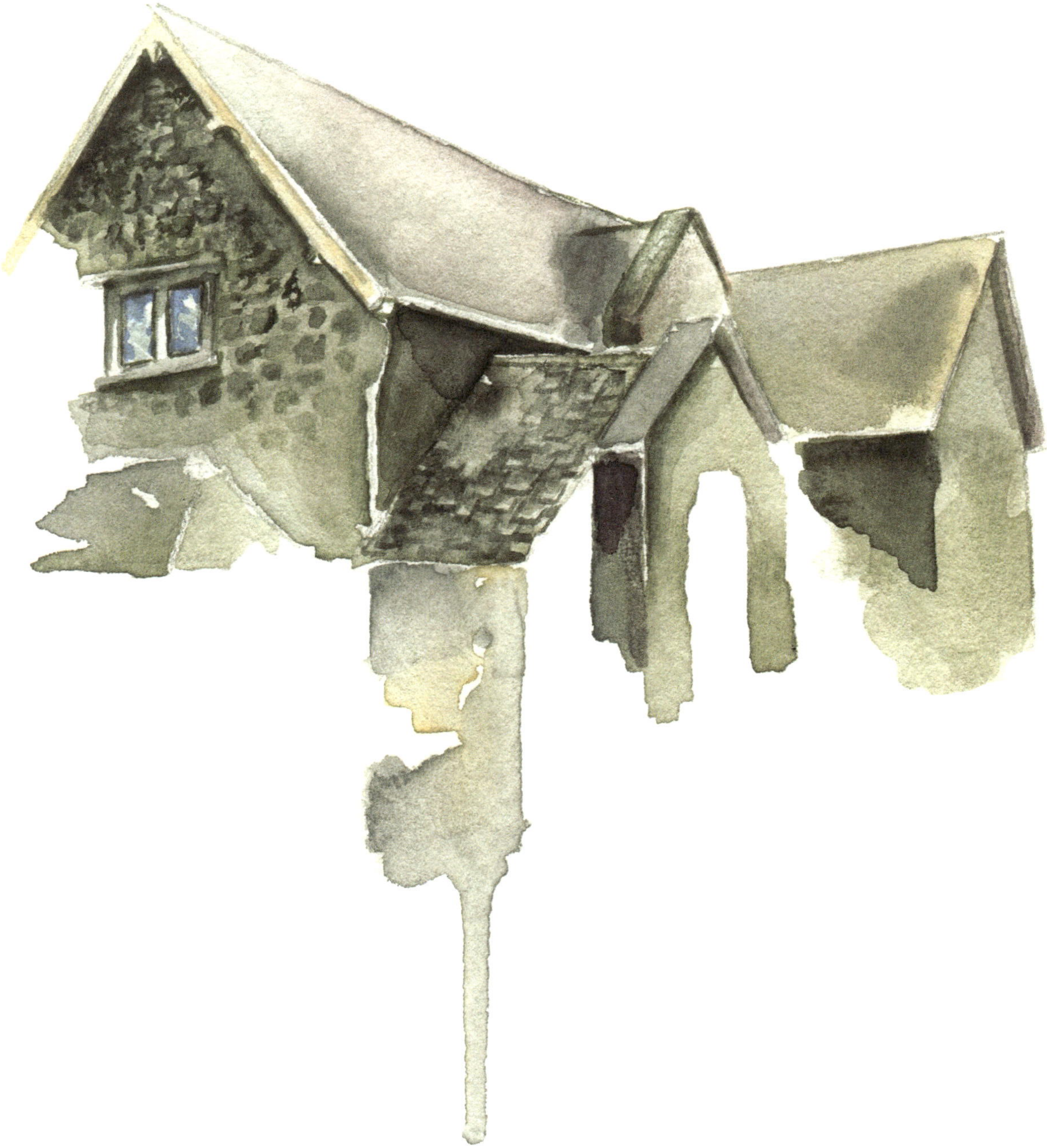

№ 4

THE COTTAGE

RECIPE FOR RIGHT PERSPECTIVE / BY ALLIE SAMPSON / PAINTING BY JUSTINA STEVENS

I used to love driving around unexplored neighborhoods with my mom. For hours we'd get lost in tucked-away subdivisions, admiring houses and praising the unique details that each one featured. My mom would slow the car down drastically just to make sure that we had enough time to savor each passing house. Occasionally, if we found one that took our breath away, she would stop altogether. It was a peculiar hobby we accidentally got swept into on our way to the grocery store or coming home from school. It quickly became one of my favorite childhood activities that I have carried with me into my adult life.

One time in my college years, my roommate and I decided to peruse undiscovered, winding subdivisions. On a small side street behind our favorite local donut shop, we came upon a charming, cozy cottage. I'm not sure what about that little house caused my heart to leap the way it did, but I suddenly found my imagination coming to life. Who lived here? What were their lives like? What would it be like to live in this darling house? Without thinking, I suddenly exclaimed, "Oh! Let's buy it!" There was something so magical, so extraordinary, about this tiny cottage. For the first time, instead of seeing a generic house, I saw a home.

I remember the first time my perspective shifted to seeing my heart as a home for God. I was in an art class, feeling nervous and intimidated. I was prompted to draw a blueprint of my heart as though it were a home for God and I to share and enjoy. At the time I was quite discouraged—my heart felt far from a home. I viewed my heart as a real fixer-upper, a weather-beaten shack with hand-me-down furniture and rag-tag decor. It certainly didn't feel like a home, and I wouldn't blame God if He wasn't interested in spending time there. This was how I saw myself and my current difficult season of life. Frankly, I felt like a mess. But He was patiently waiting to speak a wonderful truth into my heart.

Feeling tense, I sat with the Father and journaled His voice, asking Him what our home looked like. He came instantly. Instead of seeing an embarrassing, abandoned house, I saw a space that was under total renovation. It was messy, but full of hope. Dusty, but full of dreaming. The Father spoke to me: "Allie, I am renovating your heart. I am taking down walls that you thought were necessary. I am replacing them with an open floor plan. I am giving you a heart where you and I can be at home together." In that simple moment, all of my fear of being a mess, too in-process, chipped off of me like old, sun-dried paint. What I had seen as a wreck, He saw as His dream. What I mistook for loss, He understood as space. I was no longer the weather-beaten, embarrassing shack. I was the lovely cottage, and I was given room to grow.

Prompt: Sit with the Father. Thank Him for creating a good home in your heart. Keep thanking Him until you begin to feel confidence rise up inside of you. Then ask Him, "Father, where have I misunderstood the home you are building in me? Where have I grown impatient, shameful or resentful of the home that we have? Where do you want to update my perspective?" Repent, and let Him transform your heart and build a new way of thinking.

NO. 5

ACCESS TO WATER

RECIPE FOR SUSTAINABILITY / BY JD GRAVITT / PHOTO BY GINNY CORBETT

"That day Isaac's servants came and told him about the well they had dug. They said, 'We've found water!'" (Genesis 26:32, NLT).

We live in a culture with a "water-bottle" mentality. Often, we expect water to be easily accessible. We can get whatever kind of water we want almost as quickly as we think, "I'm thirsty." This is quite a different mentality than that of digging your own well. Digging a well is a time-consuming process. It is a work of perseverance. Dirt and dust stand between you and the water. However, the reward of this hard work is an everlasting, dependable water source that will never run dry. The reward is sustainability for your life.

We miss the value of hard work, patience and faith if we approach God as solely an immediate "water-bottle" God. There is something special the Lord does in us when we take the time to "work until completion" like He does (Philippians 1:6). When we are thirsty for Him, the Holy Spirit oftentimes shows up in our lives in work clothes and with a shovel in hand. He is ready to dig a well in us that takes time, but that well will sustain our thirst forever. He is ready and eager to get involved with the mundane areas of our lives that very few people will ever see, like parenting, grocery shopping, paying bills, mowing the lawn or simply resting at home.

David was able to stand before the giant Goliath because he had already taken the time and energy to defeat the lion and the bear (I Samuel 17:36). He dug a well of victory in sheep fields by doing the hard work of a shepherd. He meditated in stillness on being the Beloved of God, and he actively defended his flocks. When he stepped on the battlefield, he accessed this "water of victory" in the moment for himself and for Israel.

Prompt: We have the chance to be like David. Pray, "God, please help me dig my own well with you. I accept your invitation to live a life with constant access to you and victory. Where do I start?" Listen to His voice. Write down God's response, and begin to access the "living water" of Jesus that is inside of you (John 4:14).

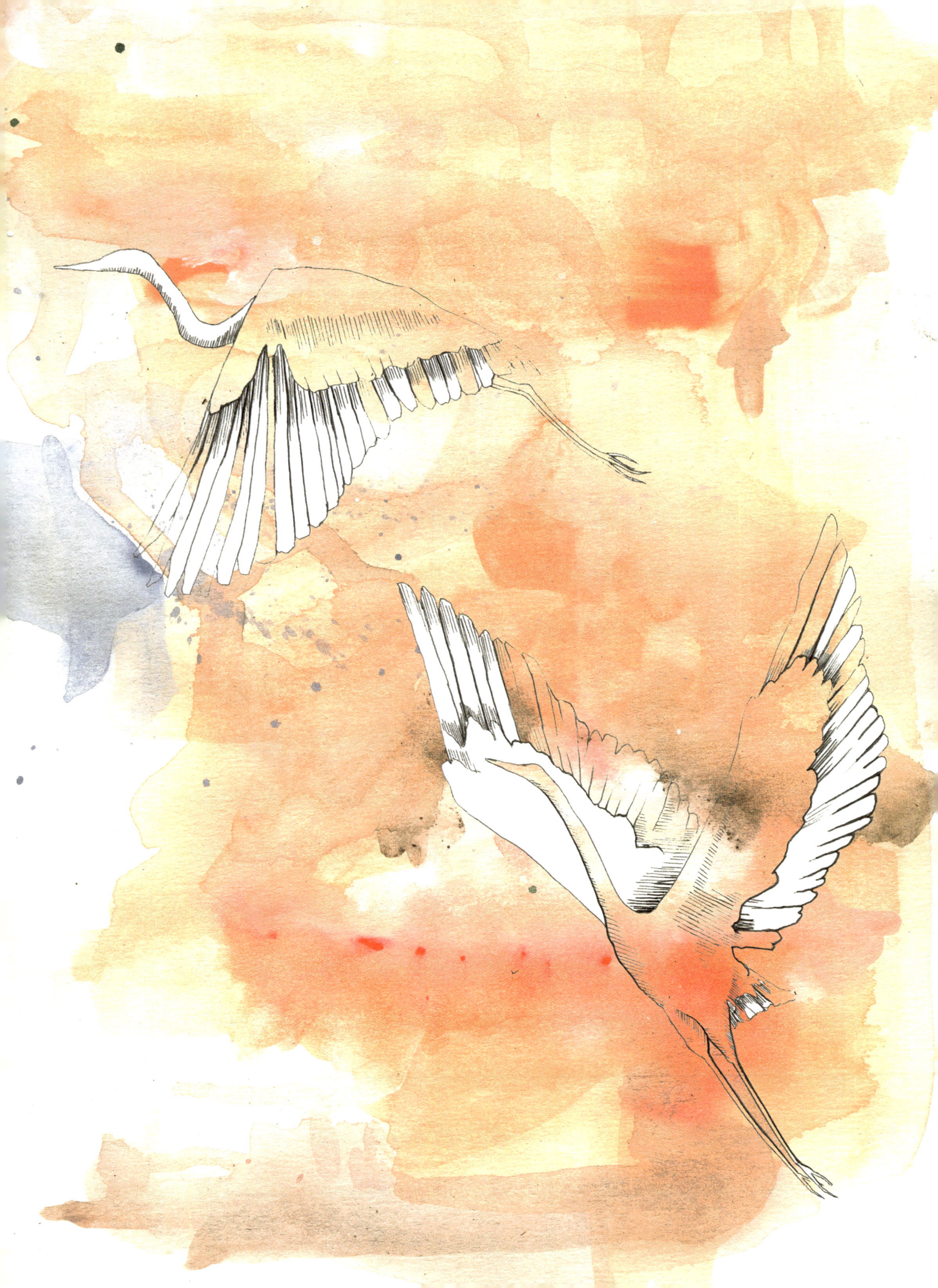

Cranes

BY MELISSA HELSER
PAINTING BY JUSTINA STEVENS

I saw a crane fly over open water,
circling, swirling, looking for a place to land,
a place to rest.
In a space surrounded by tall trees of
pine and oak and maple,
a shoreline like that of a strange circle,
surrounding it on all sides.

Its massive, wide open wings flap and fly
and come to a slow-motion stop on
a single log sticking up from the depths.
Why, in such an expanse of woods,
dry land everywhere,
would you choose the tiny log
in the middle of all uncertainty?
I don't know your heart,
what makes you come alive.

I see you from afar and marvel at how large
your wings are,
how graceful you move and breathe
over the waters.
You don't seem to strive,
patient you fly.
Your wings are bigger than I thought,
up and down they move.

It's a dance and a symphony,
I am caught in the magnificent beauty.
I sit and am overcome.
The tears fall
when it is real.
When it is a Heaven-kissing-Earth moment,
they always come.
They fall in rhythm of your beauty,
in the rhythm of your soaring and stopping.

It is there I watched you for hours,
you never moved.
You never moved.
I waited, you stayed.
And then
in deep exaltation, you lifted off.
I watched your beauty lift in white open glory.

Your wings are bigger than I thought.
I feel as if I am alive,
alive because I could see,
see a moment that usually passes quickly.
We were all in slow-motion
this day on the lake.
I will never forget how you chose
what I would never choose.

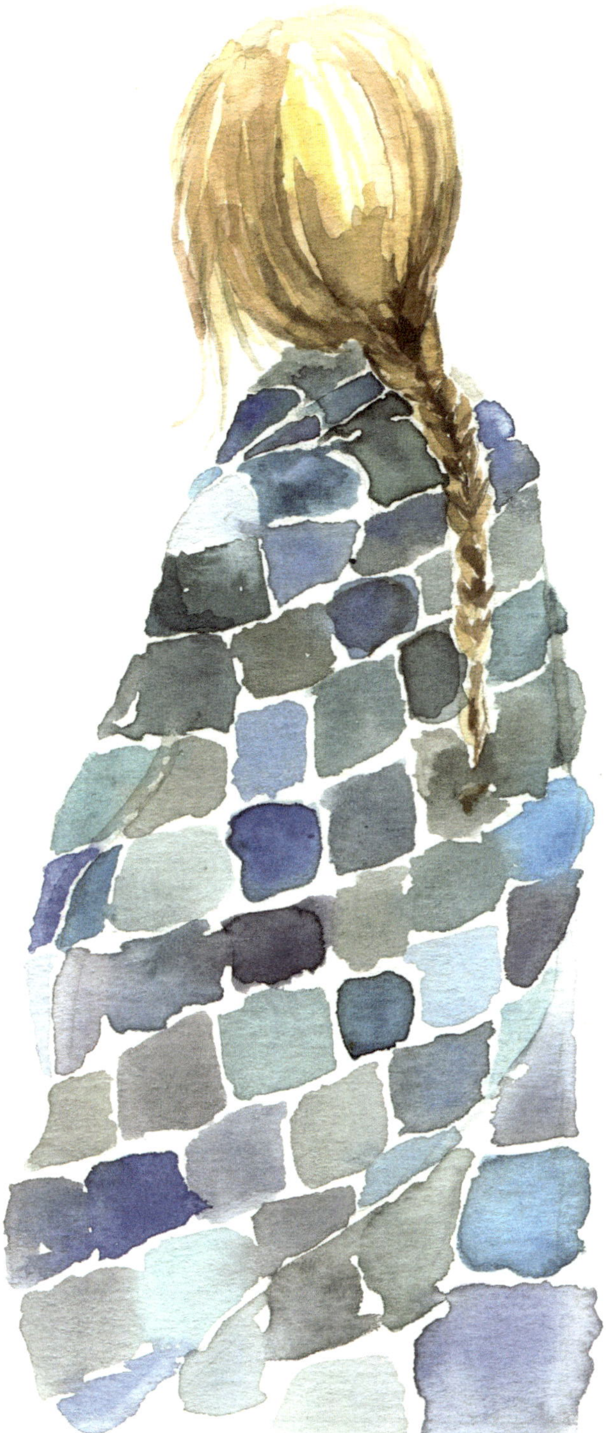

NO. 6

BLANKET OF TRUST

RECIPE FOR OVERCOMING COMPARISON / BY BRIGITTE BELL / PAINTING BY JUSTINA STEVENS

"You keep him in perfect peace whose mind is stayed on you because he trusts in you. Trust in the Lord forever, for the Lord God is an everlasting rock" (Isaiah 26:3-4, ESV).

I sit down at the piano one blustery afternoon. I begin to play. I'm resuming my efforts to master this skill of moving fluidly with both hands. As I relax and my shoulders settle, I feel the familiar whispers of defeat creep up my spine: "You are twenty-five years old and so far behind. You will never catch up. You are wasting your time." Flashes of others enter my mind, those who are excellent in their craft. Ah yes, comparison. I know you all too well. You are the robber of joy, silencer of dreams, creativity's nemesis.

I feel anger rise in my heart, "ENOUGH!" I know this creepy crawly. It's fear masked with yet another name. Comparison today, insecurity last week, pride, shame, frustration. Trace them back, and are they not all fear? Fear of failure; fear that I am not enough? Give it any name. It is the same old pillager that has been coming my whole life long in one costume or another.

Is the antithesis of my enemy not trust?

Trust.

I pause, my fingers mid-scale. I sit up a little taller. It is a simple moment of practice; of choosing the discipline to learn, and I find myself in a war zone. Fear on the prowl to shut down my development, yet I remember trust. I lift my gaze to the Father. I remember the choice I have. I remember what He told me. "Trust is wrapping around your life like a blanket. It keeps out the cold and keeps in the warmth. Trust is faith. Faith is trust. You don't always have to feel trust for the choice to be real. Just as when you put on a blanket, it takes time before you actually get warm. Will you make the trade for the blanket of simple trust? It's hard to laugh and move freely when you're cold to the bone. Will you trust me?"

Yes! My answer is yes! I will make the trade. I repent for fear and wrap the blanket of trust around my shoulders once again. I surround my heart with remembrance of what my Father says about me. This is what I choose. My fingers begin to move up and down the keys again. Do I feel different than just two minutes before? Is the war over and the enemy silent? The answer is no, but the difference now is that I have made a choice. I am acting in obedience to that choice. My fingers touch white then black, black then white. I keep my gaze on His face, and yes, here it comes—the warmth. It starts slow in my fingers and climbs up my arms until it warms my very core. Yes, He always comes.

Prompt: Ask the Holy Spirit to show where you have let fear rob you of doing something you love. Journal a prayer of repentance for agreeing with fear. Give the Father space to speak over you. Sit with His words, and let trust warm you.

SATURATED IN KINDNESS

RECIPE FOR TRYING SOMETHING NEW / BY JESSIE PHILLIPS / PHOTO BY SYDNEE MELA

"How sweet are your words to my taste, sweeter than honey to my mouth!" (Psalm 119:103, NIV).

Over the past few years I have started making honey in my own backyard. The world of bees and beekeeping was totally foreign to me. However, I've always been amazed by the diligent, hard work of bees to create sustenance of such sweet reward. With that initial spark of interest, I did some homework. I discovered that the largest bee supplier in North Carolina was one town over! I excitedly bought hives and supplies from them and ordered one colony (10,000 bees).

I'll never forget the feeling I felt when I was five months pregnant and that huge package arrived on our doorstep: "Oh my gosh, this is for real!" It contained all the essentials I needed to start setting up my hives. I was eager after months of preparing and researching bees. Somehow I still felt like I knew nothing, but I was ready to get my hands sticky. I donned the bee suit (amazingly my baby bump fit under it), which protected my face and body from stings. I felt nervous but happy under the heavy cloth layer, dreaming about joining hands with the Creator of Heaven and Earth in caring for my bees and cultivating sweet honey to eat.

Honeybees are evidence that God is acutely detailed. Each bee in the hive has a specific role in the process of making honey. Bees know how to make perfectly hexagonal cells. They know when to fan nectar with their wings to create the thick golden substance; they know when and how to preserve each comb of sweetness. All of these roles are not taught to them, but they are instinctive. Honey is a healing aid, very rich in nutrients, and it is the only food source that never spoils in edible form.

The process of harvesting the first batch of honey took an entire two years of hard work. After months of diligence and commitment to my bees, finally approaching the harvest seemed surreal. Nervous and excited to start, I felt overwhelmed with the reality that I was a beginner. I had no idea what I was doing, no idea which approach would be best in harvesting. I set up a gravity extractor on my kitchen counter. At the time, I didn't know that using a gravity extractor actually takes more time. What could happen in moments with other techniques takes weeks with this approach. I quickly began to grow anxious. Why was it so slow? What was taking so long? Would anything come out of all of my hard work? It wasn't long before these questions sent a rush of apprehension over me. Suddenly, I took matters into my own hands and began scraping and squeezing the honey from the combs. I made a massive mess! I was covered from fingertips to shoulders in thick, sticky gold, but my heart was covered in pure joy. I couldn't believe it. Real honey! Real honey from my bees! Immediately I gathered glass jars and bottles and began depositing the liquid gold inside for friends and family. I couldn't wait to let the ones I love taste what I'd given a season of my life to. As I squeezed the honey from the combs into the individual glass jars, I felt pride and accomplishment fill me up. Just like the liquid gold that was dripping into the jars, the sweet delight of a dream come true filled my heart.

There have been so many moments this past year where I've found myself full of apprehension and anxiety, just like I felt when I processed my first batch of honey. Moments when I've asked myself, "Was all this hope for nothing? Will anything come out of all my effort?" Then I remember that first harvest when the sweet, sticky substance nearly covered my entire being, and suddenly, all of my questions and anxiety dissolve. When I look back at that moment, I see the Father showing me that His kindness is just like that honey. When I go to harvest His kindness, it is like liquid gold that covers me from head to toe, and my entire disposition changes. Instead of questioning and becoming anxious, I end up becoming a joyful participant—hands immersed in His goodness, totally drenched in joy. When I go to meet His kindness, I am always met by an abundance that fills up jar after jar in my heart. It is a kindness that never spoils—a kindness whose nutrients will carry me through the winter.

Prompt: The Father is excited to meet you in the risks you take. Ask Him for an idea of a risk to take that involves getting your hands dirty. Maybe He's inviting you to nurure a tomato plant. Perhaps He's encouraging you to cook a new dish or play with clay. Before you begin, ask Him, "Father, how do you want to meet me with kindness in this process? How do you want to match my risk with your goodness?" Listen to what He has to say, and then enjoy making a beautiful mess while you encounter His kindness.

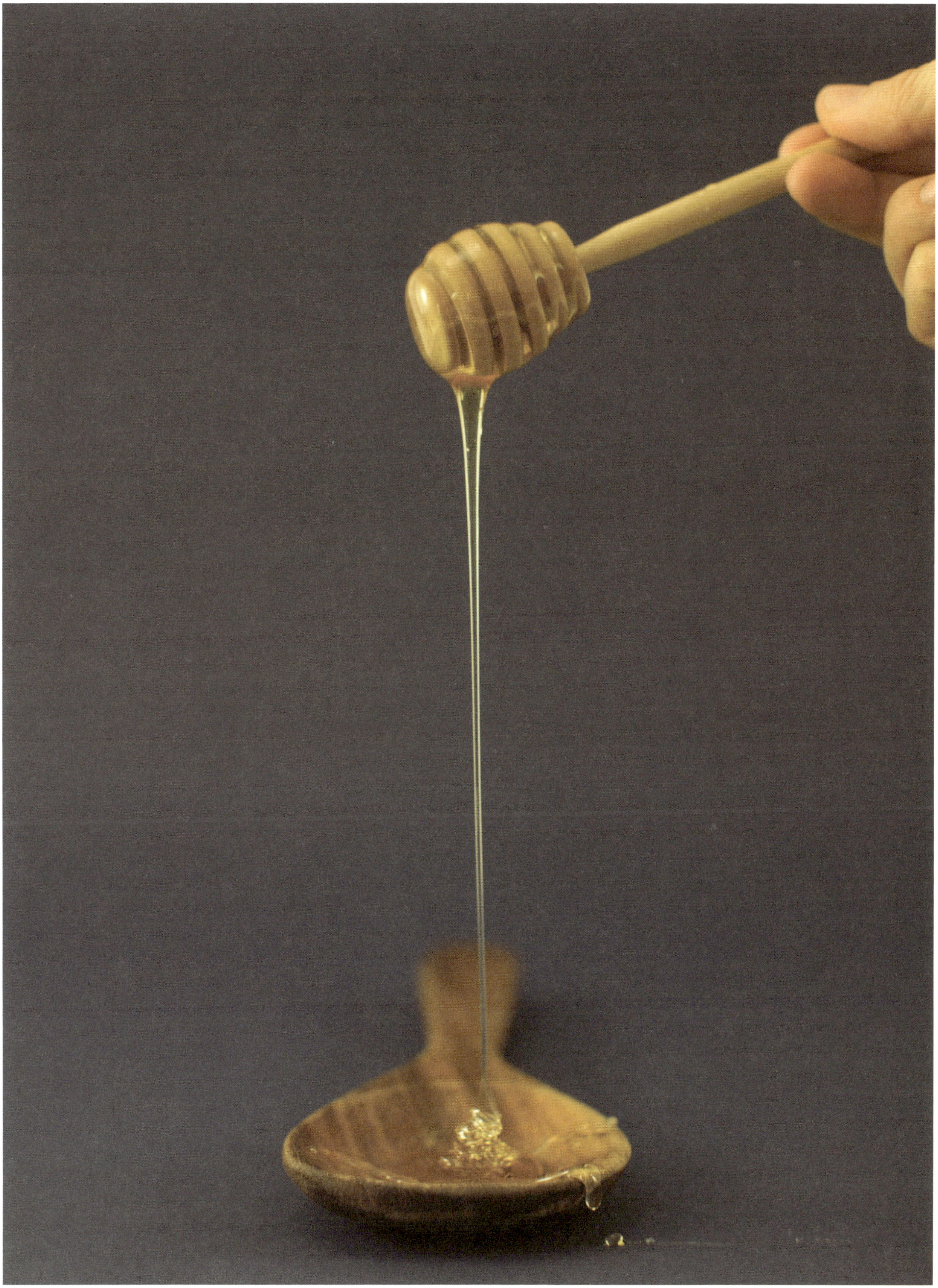

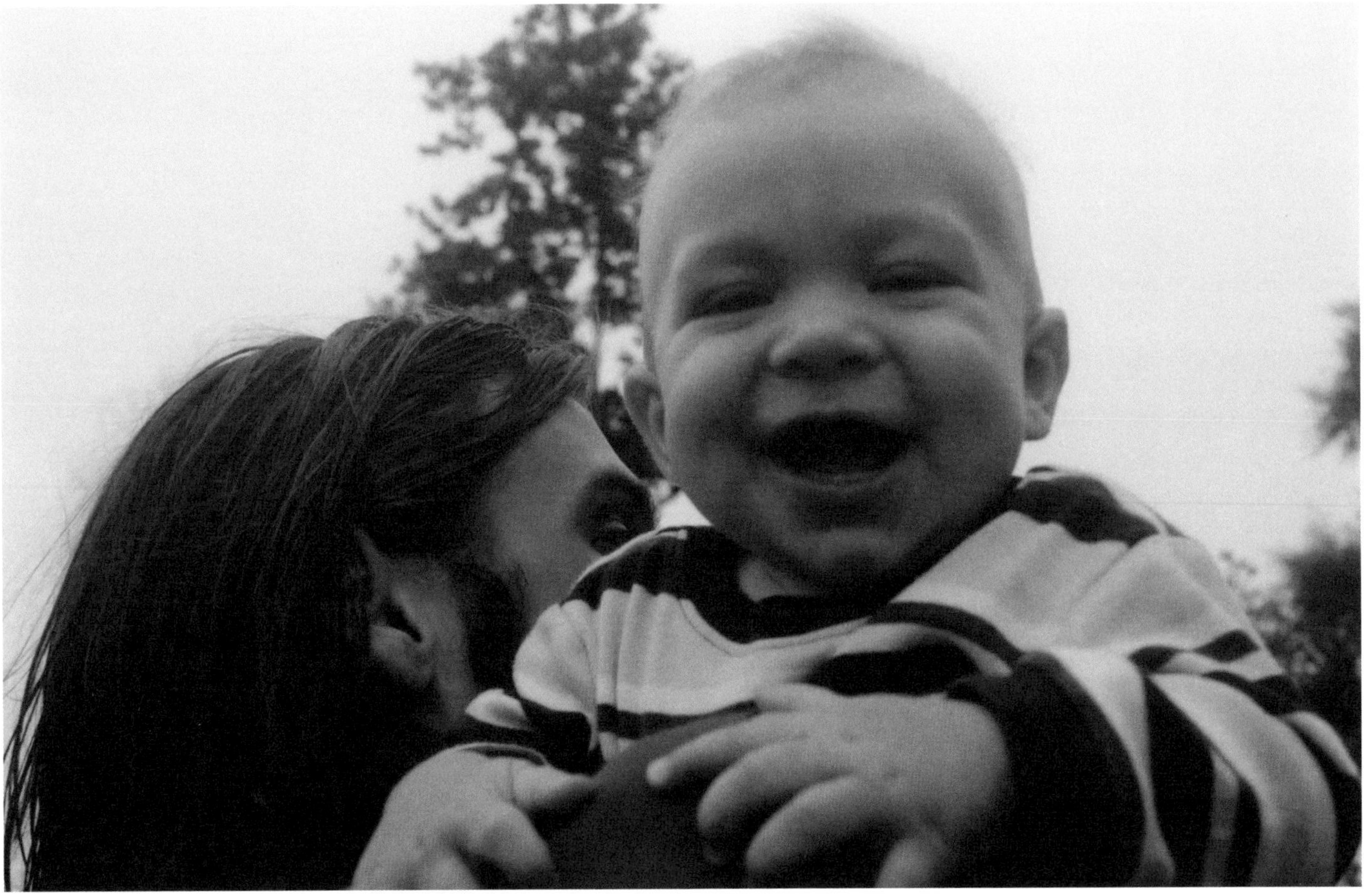

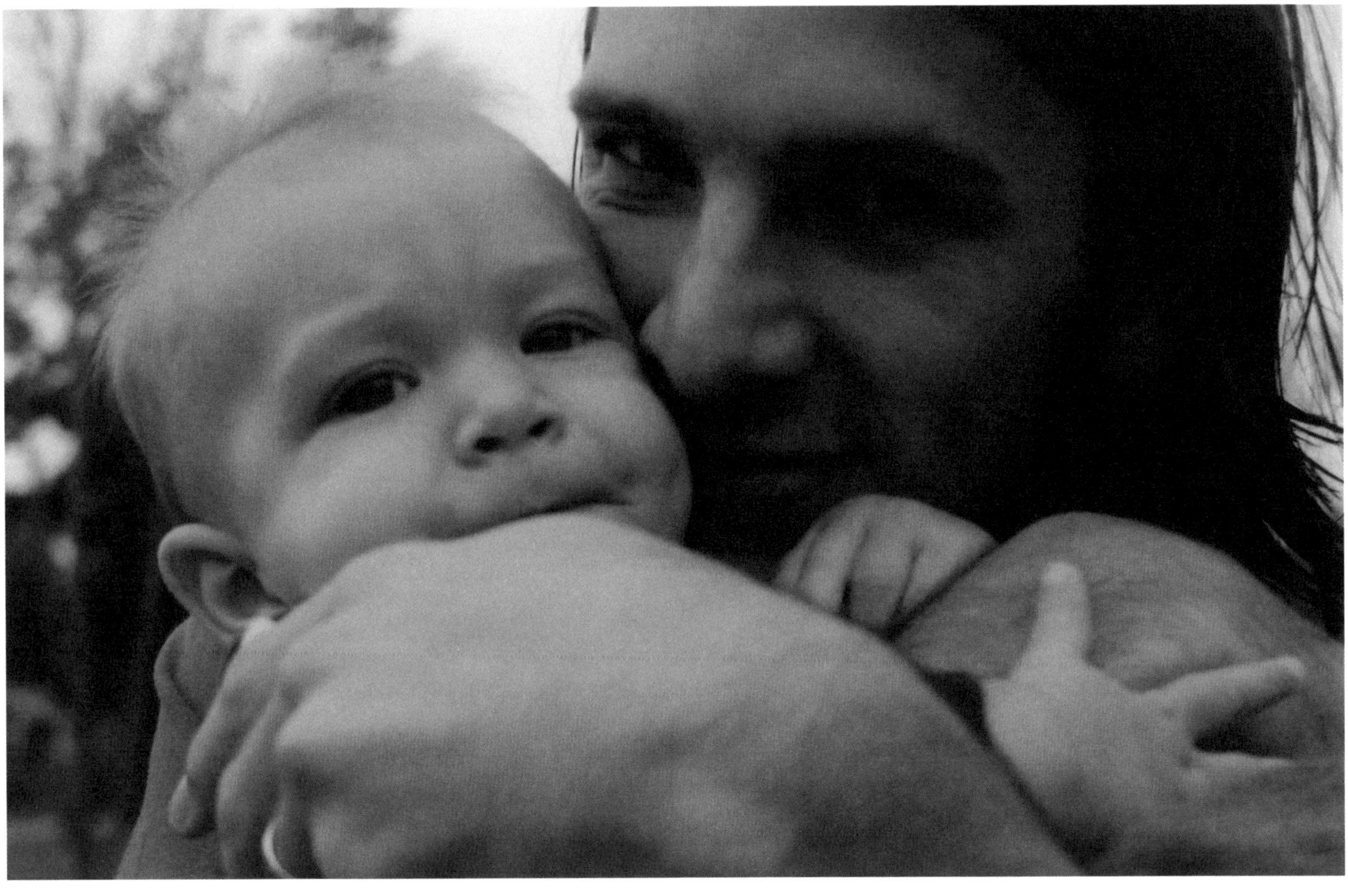

the Father's Song

BY JONATHAN DAVID HELSER
PHOTOS FROM PERSONAL COLLECTION

I couldn't wait to become a father. I can remember being a young boy dreaming about when that day would come. The desire was stirred up in me at such a young age because I had an incredible father. My dad loved me with all his heart. He wasn't perfect, but the truth is there are no perfect earthly fathers. There is only one perfect father and that is our Father in Heaven. I believe one of the greatest things we can do as parents is to lead our children to that Father. Children will outgrow their need for their earthly parents, but they will never outgrow their need for the One who is in Heaven. That's exactly where my dad led me, in his weaknesses and strengths, in his successes and failures. He pointed me to the perfect Father, and a desire was awakened in my heart.

It was only one year into marriage that Melissa and I found out we were pregnant. I will never forget the tidal wave of joy that crashed upon me that day. I remember lying in bed that evening trying my best to fall asleep, but I felt like a kid on Christmas Eve who couldn't sleep because of the anticipation of the gifts to come. My mind was flooded with the all the dreams of the kind of father I wanted to be and all that I wanted to do for this child. I was feeling the beautiful weight of the responsibility I was being given to shape my child's life with my love, affection and prayers. I could hardly believe that my child was swimming around inside my wife who was sleeping right beside me. My dreams turned into prayers as I quietly hovered my hand over Melissa's belly and began to speak over this tiny life inside her.

I remember saying something like this:

"Hello, my little gift, you don't even have ears yet, but you have a spirit and your spirit can hear this. I am already proud of you. I haven't even seen you, but you have already filled my heart and mind with delight and joy. It doesn't matter if you are a girl or boy, you have already swept me off my feet. Just the very thought of you is causing me to be filled with more love than I knew was humanly possible. I declare that you have been created by the hands of God and He has formed you to do great things. I bless you to go further than I will ever go and to change this world."

As I began to speak this, my volume began to rise and my hand rested on my sleeping wife's belly. I continued to pray for a few more moments until suddenly Melissa woke up saying, "Jonathan David, what are you doing?" (I always know I am in trouble when she says my full name.) "Why is your hand on my belly and why are you praying so loud at 2:00 in the morning? Go back to sleep, you can wait till the baby is born and then get up with him in the middle of the night as much as you want!" Over the next nine months, I will confess that I ended up waking Melissa up a couple more times with my passionate prayers and excitement. Those nine months were such a wonderful time for us as a young married couple, getting ready for our first child and preparing a home for him. One of the special things I did in that season of preparation was write a handful of songs for him. One of the songs I wrote was more than just a song, it was a prayer for his life:

Father bless this Child,
May his eyes see Your face,
May his ears hear Your voice,
May his heart love You always.

When I first wrote these lyrics, I didn't fully grasp the significance of them. That is the beauty of writing under the inspiration of the Holy Spirit. He will supersede your own ability and go beyond your own understanding. This has become more than just a song, but a crafted prayer for my children. Graham Cooke defines crafted prayer as "finding out what God wants to do and then asking him to do it." I have now been singing and praying this prayer over my children for over fourteen years, and I have realized that within these lyrics are some of my deepest core values as a parent. Let me share with you some thoughts on each line of this song:

FATHER BLESS THIS CHILD.

"Then the Lord said to Moses, 'Tell Aaron and his sons to bless the people of Israel with this special blessing: 'May the Lord bless you and protect you. May the Lord smile on you and be gracious to you. May the Lord show you his favor and give you his peace.' Whenever Aaron and his sons bless the people of Israel in my name, I myself will bless them'" (Numbers 6:22-27, NLT).

As a parent I have the same privilege as the priests to release God's blessing upon my children. This kind of prayer puts the name of God upon them. The name of God is His authority, His nature and His character. The nature of a good Father is to shower His children with blessings and to give them good things. God's first interaction with Adam in the Garden was to bless him. Before God commissioned Adam to do anything, He first blessed him. God's design is that we would complete all we do under a canopy of His blessing.

MAY HIS EYES SEE YOUR FACE.

If my children can see who God really is, it will change everything. A.W. Tozer says, "What comes into our mind when we think about God is the most important thing about us." I believe that we become what we behold, just at Paul said in II Corinthians 3:18, "But we all, with unveiled face beholding as in a mirror the glory of the Lord, are transformed into the same image from glory to glory" (NLT). The God we see is the man or woman we will be. If we see a false view of God as a fearful and angry judge, just like a mirror, our lives will reflect fear and anger. If we see the true image of God as a loving and kind Father, our lives will overflow with love, joy and kindness.

MAY HIS EARS HEAR YOUR VOICE.

One of my chief goals as a parent is to teach my children how to hear God's voice. If my kids can hear the voice of God, then they get it all. When Solomon was invited by God to ask for anything he wanted, his request was for wisdom. The Hebrew word for wisdom means a heart that hears. Because Solomon asked to hear God's voice, he got everything. I believe that Solomon had the insight to ask for wisdom because his parents had prepared him for that moment. His parents led him to the Father of fathers and that changed everything.

MAY HIS HEART LOVE YOU ALWAYS.

When we first started our journey as parents, the Holy Spirit spoke to Melissa one day and said, "The greatest thing that you can teach your children is how to love." That word has been a guiding compass to us as parents. The Scripture teaches us that we can do it all for God, but if we don't have love, we have missed it all (see I Corinthians 13). When I was growing up, my father used to say to me, "God's measuring stick for success is how much love is produced." If at the end of my life I have inspired my children and their children to love the Lord with all their hearts, then I know I have achieved eternal success.

On March 1st, 2002 around 10:30 in the evening, my firstborn son, Cadence Zion Helser, came into our world. I can't put into words how incredible that moment was. It was an explosion of emotions inside of my heart. I was smiling, I was crying, my heart was racing and it seemed like time was standing still. It was one of the most holy moments of my life seeing my son enter this world. It was truly like he was coming from Heaven into our world.

Around midnight everything had settled down in the hospital and Melissa had fallen asleep. I went over and scooped up Cadence and took him out into the hallway where I could have a moment with just my son and I. I placed Cadence on my lap, and he lay there fast asleep. He was only eight pounds, but he was the heaviest eight pounds I had ever held. The reality that this was my son was the weight I felt on my lap. I then quietly began to sing the words, "Father bless this child..." As soon as I began singing, Cadence's eyes popped wide open, and it was like he began to talk to me, not with words from his mouth, but from his heart and his spirit. This is what I heard him say:

"Oh my goodness, you're the guy! You are the guy who has been waking me and Mommy up for the last nine months—you are the voice I have been hearing. I have heard your voice my whole life, but now I see your face."

That experience I had with Cadence is picture of what it is going to be like when we pass from the womb of this world and we are born into eternal life. We are going to pass through the darkness of this Earth into the arms of a Father. In that moment we will see the face of One who has been singing over us our entire lives. I think we will exclaim just like my son did, "It's you! You are the one who has been singing over me my whole life!"

Everything in all of creation is filled with the song of the Father. On each day of creation, God stepped back from His work and sang into what He created, "It is good." The Father sang His goodness into every single thing He created. That's why you can encounter God in all of creation, from sunrises to sunsets, from mountains to oceans, from the twinkling stars above us to the tiny flowers below, all of creation echoes the melody of the Father's song. Romans 1:20 says, "For since the creation of the world God's invisible qualities—his eternal power and divine nature—have been clearly seen, being understood from what has been made" (NIV). Just as my heart was bursting with pleasure for my son before I even met him, the Father of fathers' heart was filled with delight from the moment He first thought about us. He is the one who chose us before the creation of the world, and He is the Father who has been singing over us our whole lives.

Prompt: Carve out a space of time and find a place in creation where you can step out of the noise of the world and still your soul in the beauty of nature. Remember that you are a human being before you are a human doing. God blessed us before He asked us to do anything. Let your soul be filled with this blessing, and allow your heart to fall into His arms again. Whether you walk through a forest or find a quiet park bench, whether you are on a mountain or on a beach, engage the song of the Father that is all around you. Stop and listen for it. It may be in the the rhythm of the waves or in the song the wind is playing through the leaves. Ask Him for ears to hear His song, eyes to see who He really is. His song may come in words, or it may come as a wave of gentle peace. However His song encounters you, linger in the moment and let your heart remain with the One who sang over you first.

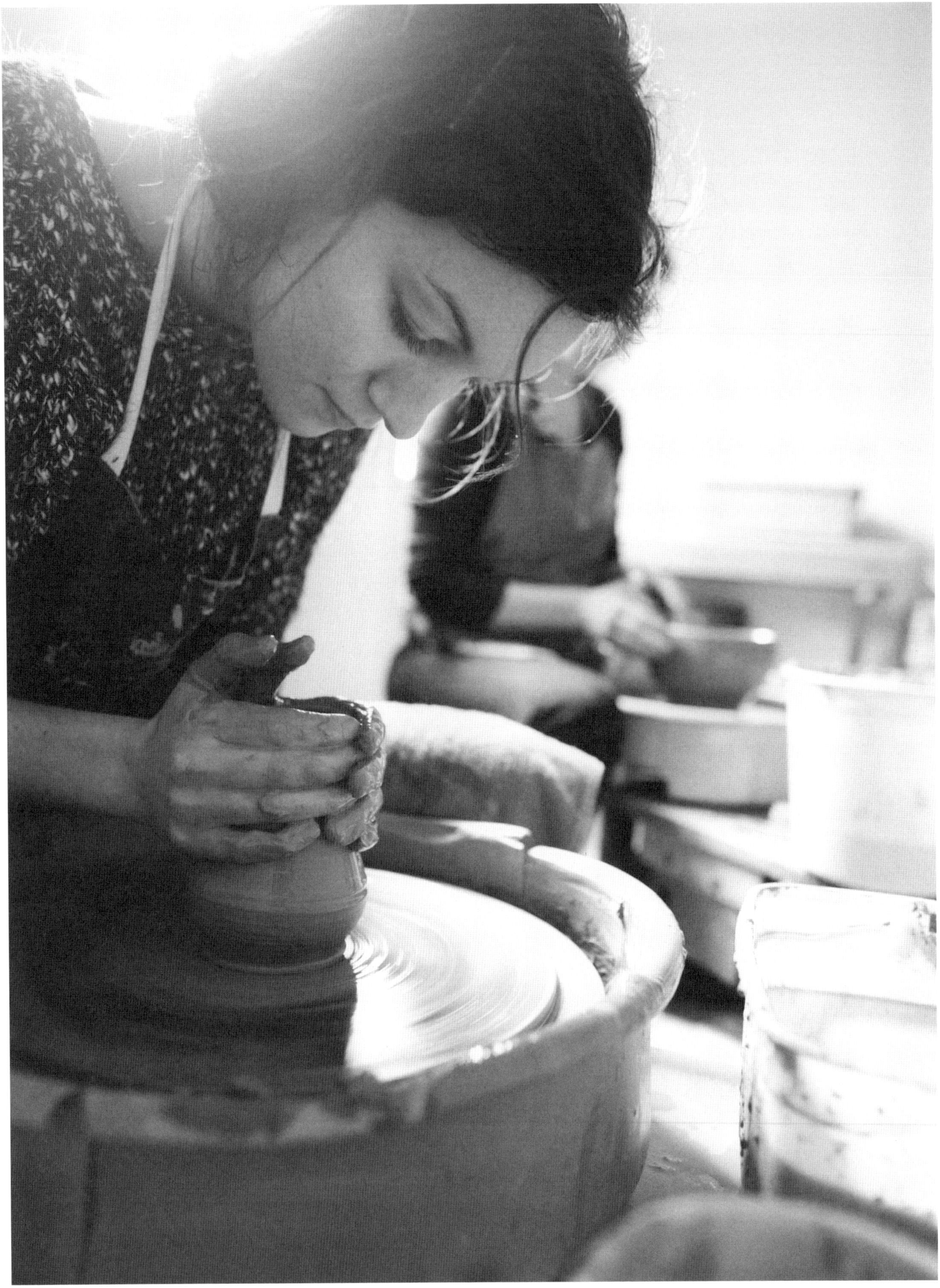

№ 8

patience in the mess

RECIPE FOR EMBRACING FAILURE
BY ROSEMARY GINGERICH / PHOTO BY SYDNEE MELA

The wheel moves at a steady pace, and I gently press into the clay to draw it up. With this particular piece, I find that the higher I draw it up, the more deformed it becomes. This must have been a fault in the centering part of the process— a crucial step that determines either the success or failure of a piece.

Every potter begins by learning how to center clay. Centering happens after you throw your ball of clay down onto the wheel and begin turning the wheel. Through a series of motions, you move the clay up and down until it comes perfectly into the center of the wheel; this is the only place on the wheel where the hands can successfully wrap around the clay and form it into a beautiful shape later on. Otherwise the spinning of the wheel will work against the hands and cause the piece to become deformed or collapse. Though this may sound easy, it is a difficult part of the process and takes a lot of practice to learn. Therefore it is inevitable that I fail; in fact, it is essential.

I remind myself of this as I feel the walls weakening on the piece I have unsuccessfully centered. Suddenly, the top of my cylinder shape caves in on itself, going from a tall, happy cylinder to a frowning lump of clay. In seasons past this would have discouraged me, angered me even, but at this point I have deformed enough pieces to know that in order to grow and keep the love of pottery alive, I must have patience to learn from my failures and keep playing.

Making space for failure is vital, because each failure brings me one step further in my skill and knowledge of a craft that truly takes a lifetime to learn. I become a little more free each time I am faced with a misshapen piece because it helps me to be less timid the next time I sit down at the wheel. Each failure has opened my eyes to see the beauty of the process of learning to create a work of art out of something that is no more than a lump of clay from the ground. Patience in failure and learning to love (and not simply tolerate) the many different parts of the process that go into making one piece has made space for the Father to reveal deeper truths about His nature to me through this craft.

Though I sometimes resist the shaping of His hands, there is grace because He is patient with me. Endlessly patient. He patiently shapes us through our successes and failures to become whole and complete. He is okay with the mess, the process; He takes it all and uses it for growth and beauty within us.

I take my hands and begin to play with the clay as the wheel continues to move. With delight in my heart, I find that this frowning lump of clay soon becomes a vase with a thin neck and opening, perfect for a small bouquet of wildflowers. I can't deny it looks slightly uneven, but there's something about its odd shape that I love. Maybe because it represents something deeper that has grown in my heart after so many collapsed pieces: the fruit of patience. Patience in the unending process and messy failures. Patience in knowing that He has been with me in my process as I turn on the wheel of life and slowly become a work of art.

Prompt: Ask the Father, "Where are areas in my life that my eyes need to be opened to see the beauty in the process of shaping? Where do I need renewed grace and patience for my own heart as you transform me into something amazing?"

NO. 9

soft clay

RECIPE FOR A SOFTENED HEART
BY EMILY PELL / PHOTO BY MORGAN CAMPBELL

Clay without the potter's hands can do nothing but remain a lump of earth. Yet even clay can resist the potter's hand and refuse to come to the center of the wheel. One day at my pottery class, an experienced potter friend watched as I tried to center a small ball of clay on the wheel. I was really struggling and growing even more frustrated as the time passed. After nearly twenty minutes of struggle, my friend came over and asked if he could help. I gratefully agreed. He touched my clay and immediately knew the problem. "This clay is too hard. It's impossible to center," he said with teacherly kindness. "You need to add water to this lump of clay and let it sit until it's absorbed the water, then you'll have a much easier time."

In the moment, I felt a tug on my heart and knew the Father wanted to tell me something. Soon after, the Holy Spirit clearly showed me that my heart was just like the clay that I couldn't center. I knew there were places in my heart that had grown hard and really needed help. In a way, I wanted God to wrestle me and make me center, even if I wasn't capable or ready. The Good Potter wasn't going to try to force my hard heart to the center of the wheel; instead, He was going to put me in a safe place where all I could do was absorb His water and let it soften my heart.

What this looked like for me was being immersed into a community of people. Each one of them carried a piece of the Father's tenderness for my heart. This community supported me as I learned to stay still and let the Father soak my heart in His love. I discovered that I had to be loved before I lifted a finger for anyone else. This took time, patience and trust. My hardness came off in layers. But what this transformation produced in me was a pliable heart, just like soft clay.

"Yet you, Lord, are our Father. We are the clay, you are the potter; we are all the work of your hand" (Isaiah 64:8, NIV). God chose to show humanity what He is like through the picture of a humble potter. The potter doesn't depend heavily on tools, only skilled hands covered in mud. The posture of a potter is not proud and disconnected; rather it is fully committed with arms strong and steady, eyes fixed and full of vision, and hands gently guiding the lump of earth into something beautiful.

God places me on the wheel with a perfect vision of what He is creating. Using both hands, He guides me to the center of the wheel. His face is close to me and my mud is on His hands. He draws me up and shapes me. He is the potter, and I am the clay.

Prompt: Imagine that you are a lump of clay on the Father's wheel. Are you soft clay, able to be sculpted by His hands? Perhaps you realize that you are like hard clay, and really need to be submersed in His love before anything gets done today. Perhaps you have been in the water a long time, and now it's time to let Him take you out of the "safe" environment and make something amazing out of you. Pray this prayer: God, I want to be soft clay, a balanced person in your hands. I repent for the places that I've resisted the water of your loving kindness. I open my hands. Come soften me, Father. Then, when you are ready, ask the Father this question and journal His response: Will you show me what beautiful thing you are ready to shape me into?

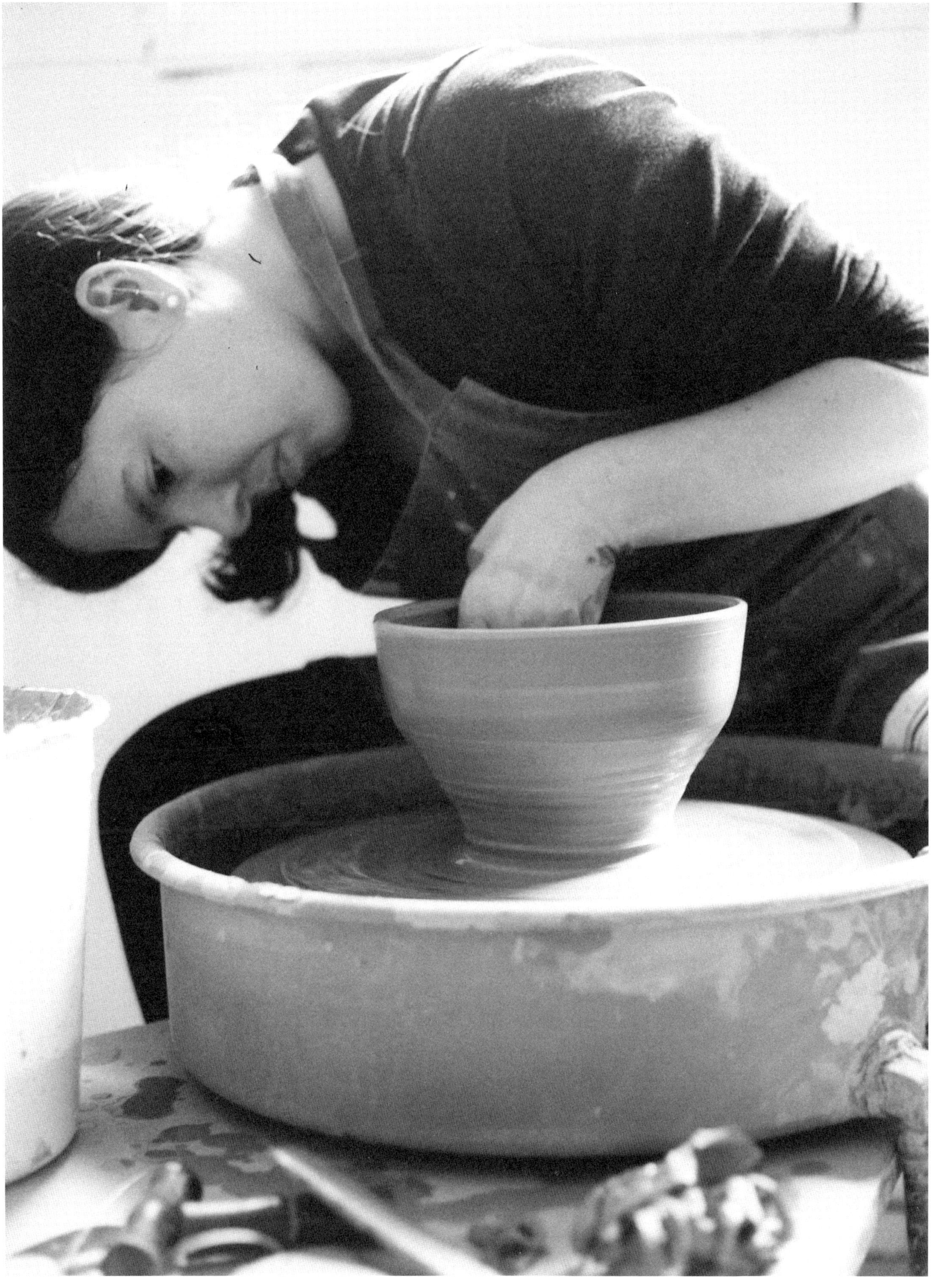

No. 10

ROOTBOUND

RECIPE FOR FORGIVENESS / BY LINDA HELSER
PAINTING BY JUSTINA STEVENS

In the spring the closest thing to Heaven on this earth for me is going to a nursery and picking out beautiful plants. I love my flower garden.

One Saturday morning my husband, Ken suggested we build a rock wall around my flowers to make them even more beautiful. I loved that idea, but quickly confessed I knew nothing about building a wall, but Ken promised to show me. Actually his idea was that he'd teach me how to mix the cement and he, the artist, would fashion the wall. I didn't care. I loved him for just wanting to give of himself to me in something that I treasured.

So off we went that morning in our old "redneck" pickup truck, affectionately called, Mighty White, to the local hardware store to gather our rock for the garden. While we were lifting the heavy stones into the truck, the owner, who knew my love for plants, came over and informed me that he had just reduced all of his nursery items fifty percent. I stepped from loading heavy rocks to standing near the gates of Heaven. And though most of the plants were getting kind of old and should have been planted months ago, I still came up with a pretty good assortment.

For the rest of that day it was some hard work, mixing cement and sand to make a mortar, and then moving a heavy wheelbarrow over to Ken who mostly stayed on his knees making each stone fit perfectly into the wall. Toward the day, the wall was finished. My precious husband, sweat pouring down his face, worked buckets of potting mix and compost into the hard red clay ground. When the soil was ready, he motioned for me to come over and plant my first flower in the hole he had carefully scooped out with his hands. I was nearly shaking with excitement. I pulled the pot away from the plant, and I found that it was the worst root bound plant I'd ever seen. So root bound it did not even need the pot. There was no loose root anywhere, just a tangle of knots. I then realized why the plants were on sale, they should have been planted way before the middle of July. This plant was so tangled there was no way it would ever root in the ground. I stared hopelessly at the plant.

God began to address my heart. Before any of this had happened, I asked God to show me a picture of what forgiveness looked like. I didn't expect for my answer to come while I had dirt all over my hands, doing something as ordinary as planting flowers, but it did. I heard God speak: "You asked me to show you a picture of forgiveness. But sometimes you discover what something is by what it's not. This is not a picture of forgiveness, but unforgiveness. When anyone refuses to forgive, they become root bound, ingrown with bitterness, and hard of heart…"

His voice was crystal clear, and I felt answered. I could see what unforgiveness truly was: a life the shape of ugly, selfish, bitter knots. No matter where the plant is put and no matter how good the soil it is planted in, it will always remain a single flower and never ever produce more flowers. It would always remain a root bound plant, unless I did something.

I reached for a sharp knife to cut at the roots and pull them apart, I immediately realized what happened in my life many years ago when I gave my life to Jesus and I said yes to forgiveness. The Holy Spirit of the Living God reached into my heart that could have remained root bound, and cut away at me, not to hurt me but to free me. Free me from my own root bound prison that I could have remained in for the rest of my life. On my knees in the dirt before a root bound plant I cried, "Jesus, Jesus, Jesus. Thank you for giving me the great grace and love to forgive. Oh God, thank you for cutting away my rights to feel sorry for myself and pulling me apart to dependence on You, and planting me down deep in the soil of your own heart."

Forgiveness does not necessarily mean that everything will change and become different, for often the one whom you offer forgiveness does not receive it. But does that matter? Forgiveness' beauty lies in the fact that you are changed. Set free. The past is under the blood of Christ and you don't have to dig it up. You bury it. Forgiveness means you no longer hold onto the past, and the past can no longer hold onto you.

Prompt: Take a minute and look at the painting of the root bound plant. Think about a place in your life that is like a beautiful plant on the top but below is tangled in roots of unforgiveness, selfishness or fear. Imagine yourself holding that plant. Hold your hands out just like you're holding that plant in real life and hand it over to God. Let Him come in with a sharp knife and untangle the mess. Pray this prayer, "God, cut away my rights to feel sorry for myself, I choose dependency on you, Father. Amen"

NO. 11

IN THE EARLY HOURS

PROMPT BY MEGHAN HOCKADAY

There's something especially sweet about the first few hours of morning. Everything around you is waking up: morning dew glistens in greeting, sun's rays lazily spill over windowsills and paint bedroom walls in a gentle wash of light. The first moments of the day are sometimes the most precious, centering our hearts and preparing us for what lies ahead. These moments also have a tendency to become the most routine. We go through movements of comforting familiarity to awaken our senses once again to the world around us. This could be as simple as the way you cook your eggs, how much cream or sugar goes in your tea, even your morning commute. The Holy Spirit loves to meet us in the mountain-top moments of wild worship and powerful teaching, but there is something in the simple everyday that is so sacred to Him. Jesus spent thirty years of His life, mostly undocumented, living this everyday. He was just as enchanted with the world around Him during those thirty years as He was in the last three years of His life on Earth. He spent many mornings soaking in the beauty around Him and many evenings sitting at a table with His best friends, enjoying life together.

Think of a rhythm you practice every morning. Invite the Holy Spirit into the simplest of things—how you make your breakfast or where you go to sit and spend time with Him. Breathe in the beauty of beginning your day in this still, quiet space.

"Let me hear of your unfailing love each morning, for I am trusting in you. Show me where to walk, for I give myself to you" (Psalm 143:8, NLT).

NO. 12

IN THE EVENING

PROMPT BY MORGAN CAMPBELL

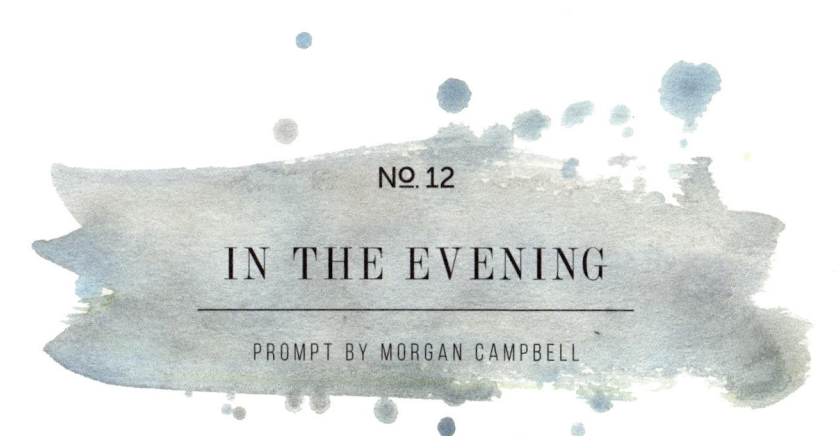

I recently visited The Metropolitan Museum of Art in New York City, one of the most beautiful and inspiring places I have encountered. Wandering from room to room, I stopped to rest on a big marble bench and found myself staring at the brush strokes of Roses by Vincent Van Gogh. Reading the date on the plaque below, I was struck that 125 years later, I was able to encounter the same beauty Van Gogh experienced in the shape of a vase and the form of a flower.

In that moment, I realized every glimpse of beauty is a mirror that reflects the face of the Creator. God is the founder of color, the One who paints the deep blue of the ocean and the spots on a fawn. He made beauty to point to His intentionality; He made it for our pleasure and delight.

"The eye is the lamp of the body. So, if your eye is healthy, your whole body will be full of light" (Matthew 6:22, ESV).

We are made by the Creator. Practice finding the Holy Spirit's fingerprints right under your nose. I love slowing down long enough in the evening to admire the the sun's light and shadows. You can collect the moments and record the colors and shapes you see in your journal with watercolors or ink. At the end of your day, craft an intentional prayer and thank the Father for His omnipresent goodness and beauty in your everyday life.

Begin the ascent

"HE THREW HIS ARMS AROUND HIM, LAVISHED ATTENTION ON HIM, GUARDING HIM AS THE APPLE OF HIS EYE. HE WAS LIKE AN EAGLE HOVERING OVER ITS NEST, OVERSHADOWING ITS YOUNG, THEN SPREADING ITS WINGS, LIFTING THEM INTO THE AIR, TEACHING THEM TO FLY."

DEUTERONOMY 32:10-11, MSG

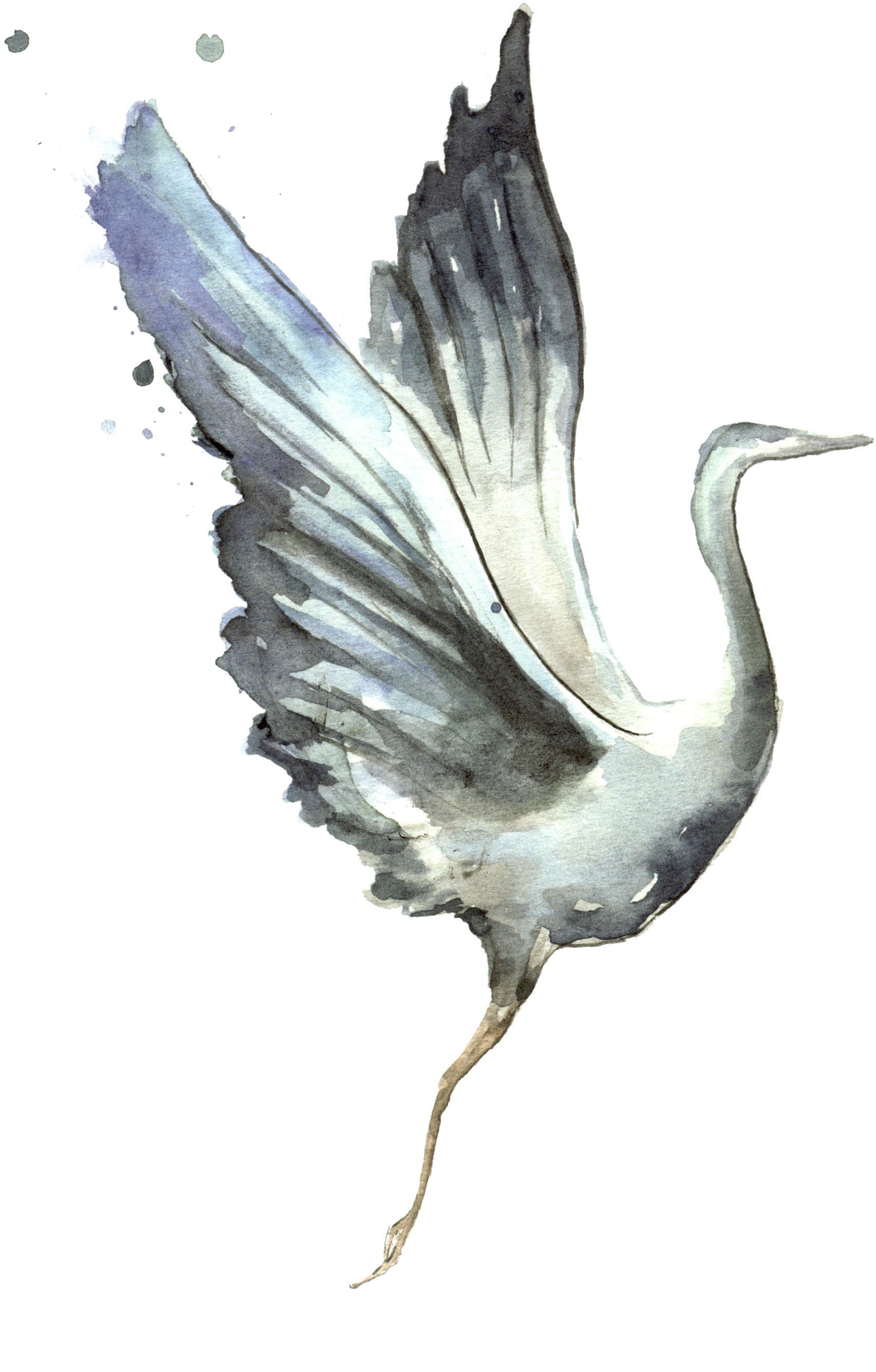

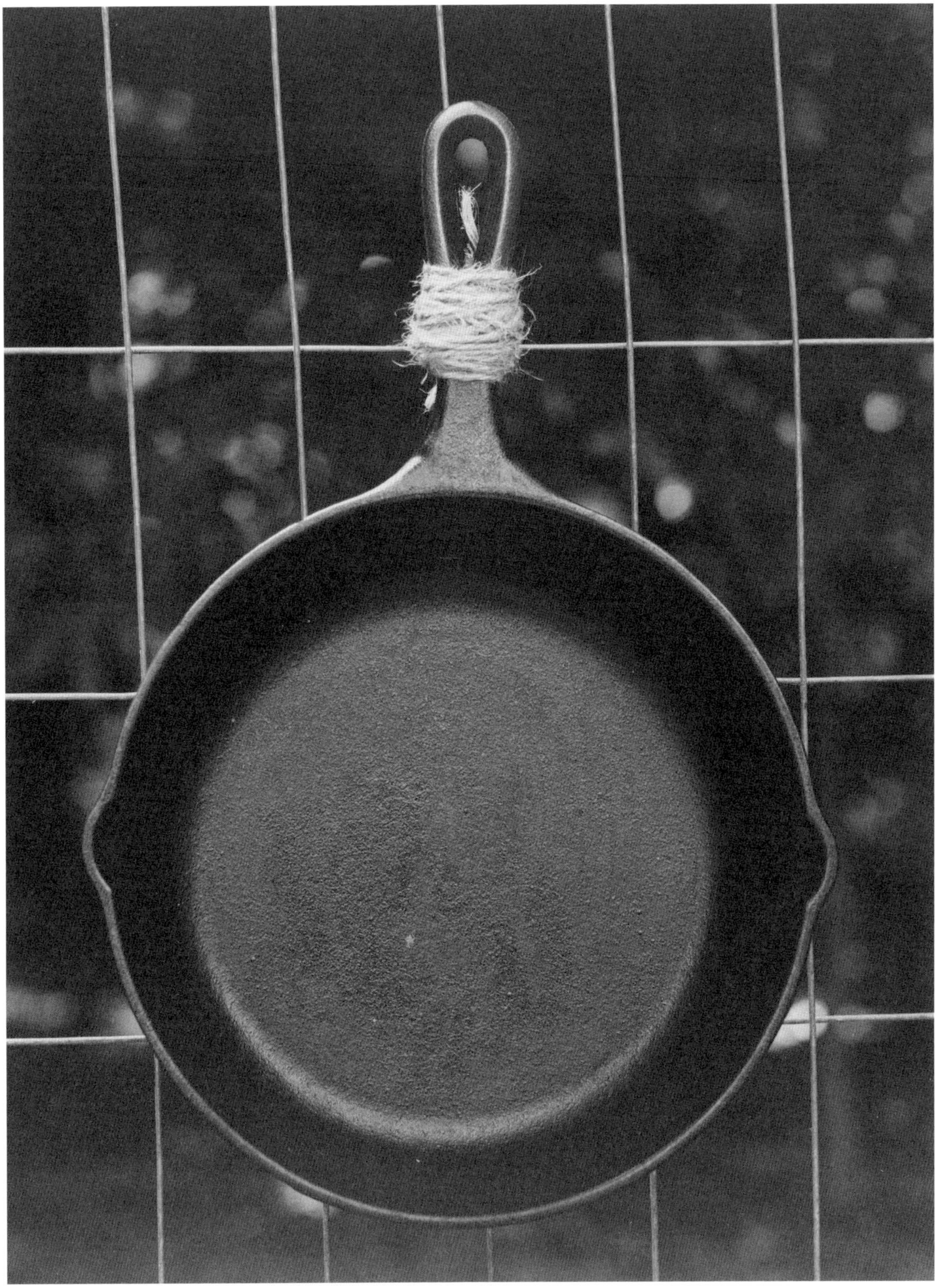

NO. 13

SEASONING A
CAST IRON SKILLET

RECIPE FOR RESTORATION / BY CHRIS MILLER
PHOTO BY SYDNEE MELA / ILLUSTRATIONS BY LINDSAY VANCE

Of all the gifts and housewares that line the cupboards and fill the drawers of our home, there are few things that I'd really hate to part with. A sixty-year-old cast iron skillet with the number eight inscribed on the handle is one such item. I have fond childhood memories of my grandmother frying chicken and baking cornbread in cast iron pans. To this day, there's nothing like the intoxicating aroma of collard greens or the sweet scent of her homemade preserves simmering on the stovetop. In my grandparents' house, the same old kitchen countertop greets me each time I enter—the countertop that I sat at for sandwiches in the summer, cookies at Christmastime and holiday ham carved by my grandfather.

A few years back, my grandmother opened a cabinet underneath that countertop and pulled out her old skillet with "8" on the handle. It was blackened with layers of memories. She handed it to me and said, "This belonged to my mother, but I haven't used it in a long time. See what you can do with it." I examined the heirloom gift and considered its lifetime of wear. It was caked with old grease, which told me exactly where to begin.

The next day, I spent the afternoon outside collecting fallen tree limbs with my grandfather, piling them into the back of his old red pickup truck for firewood. After we had built a significant pile, I took the old cast iron pan, turned it upside down and placed it in the heart of what would soon become a glorious fire. The next day I returned to a pile of ash. There in the center I found my gift gleaming in the noonday sun. The once charred instrument had been restored to its raw form. The now smooth and silvery surface revealed the craftsmanship of the cast iron.

My mission was to re-season the newly restored pan to its greatest potential. I spent time researching and crafting a vision for my newfound treasure. I learned about the science of seasoning and purchased the best type of oil to protect and seal the surface. Layer by layer I learned that the process of preheating, coating, baking and cooling was one of patience and intention. There were no shortcuts. Each step was instrumental in working toward a beautiful, long-lasting finish. The process required my full attention. There were times when I was tempted to rush the process. Sometimes I wanted to use more oil than was recommended, and other times I considered shortening the time in the oven. But had I rushed, I would have encouraged an uneven cooking surface and could have ruined the entire seasoning process. In doing so, I was able to re-season the pan into a powerful and effective cooking vessel.

Many of us feel like the old cast iron skillet my grandmother gave me. Our once valuable hearts have become hardened, caked with distrust and rusted from neglect or overuse. The Father has come to recover your life. He sees the value in your well-casted heart. He says, "I can do something with this." In fact, He says, "I can do exceedingly and abundantly more than they can ask or imagine with this!" It takes careful planning to build a healthy foundation. The Father is ready to walk with you through the steps it requires to burn away all that has been and prepare you for all that is to come. He is patient. He does not skip steps. He longs to restore you to your true identity and purpose. Will you say yes?

HOW *to* SEASON YOUR SKILLET

Find a good cast iron skillet. Examine its size and shape. How does it feel in your hand? You want to find one that you'll love and use for years to come. Look for an old one, something with a story. Your goal will be to strip your pan down to bare iron and start fresh, seasoning it from scratch, one layer at a time.

Chances are your old pan is covered in layers of grit and grime. That might seem charming, but it will not yield well in your seasoning process. The goal is to restore and seal it with a protective coating that will double as an amazing cooking surface. The two ways to do this are by fire or oven. If you have the ability to build a decent fire, you can turn the pan upside down and place it in the heart of the flame. Surround the pan with coals to get it hot enough to burn down to bare iron. Don't worry about it melting; your skillet can take the heat. If building a fire is not an option for you, you can also use a standard oven on the self-cleaning cycle. This will also get hot enough to burn down to bare iron, though it may also produce a fair amount of smoke. Both of these methods may require a second treatment, depending on the severity of the build-up. Remember, your goal is burn away the old to prepare for the new.

Once you have burned your pan down to expose bare iron, you are ready for the process of seasoning. You will need the following:

- An oven
- A bottle of raw, unfiltered flax seed oil (This is found in the refrigerated section of your local health food store or natural grocery. Check the date; this oil can go rancid easily.)
- A clean cloth or a roll of paper towels to apply oil to your pan

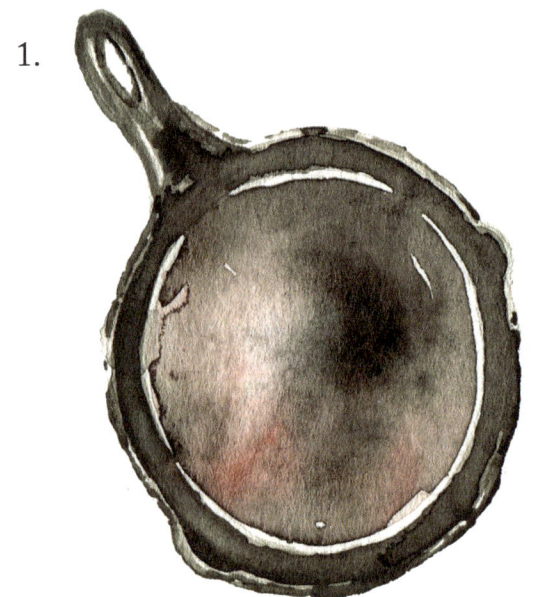

1.

Place your cast iron skillet inside a cool oven. With the pan inside, bring the oven to 200 degrees Fahrenheit. This will warm the pan and open its pores.

2. Remove the pan from the oven. Pour unfiltered flaxseed oil (cold-pressed) onto a clean cloth or paper-towel. Generously coat the entire pan with the oil, inside and out. Immediately wipe off ALL of the visible oil. The porous cast iron has now absorbed all that it needs for its first season. The surface should be smooth and appear fairly dry with no excess oil. Turn the pan upside down and place back inside the warm oven.

3. Bring the oven to 450 - 500 degrees Fahrenheit. Once the oven reaches its target temperature, set a timer for one hour. Leave the pan to bake and season.

4. After one hour, turn off the oven. Allow the pan inside to cool for two to three hours, leaving the oven door closed.

5. Repeat this process seven times. You can begin the next coat as soon as the pan and the oven have cooled to at least 200 degrees.

6. After you have seasoned your pan, cooking with a fat such as butter or oil is still recommended. In time, your pan will increase in its non-stick capabilities. To sustain the life of your pan, do not use soap on your seasoned skillet. This can damage your seasoning. Instead, use hot water and a clean scrub brush to clean. Coarse salt is very beneficial in assisting with scrubbing your pan after heavy use. You have worked hard to season your pan; care for it, and it will serve you well!

№ 14

SYMPATHY VS. EMPATHY

RECIPE FOR EMPATHY / BY JUSTINA STEVENS / PHOTO FROM PERSONAL COLLECTION

"For we do not have a high priest who is unable to empathize with our weaknesses, but we have one who has been tempted in every way, just as we are—yet he did not sin" (Hebrews 4:15, NIV).

I remember so clearly my feet hitting the sand; I laughed and squealed as I held my dad's hand. I was a little girl running—shifting my short legs like scissors, my dad taking steady, slow-paced steps to match my own. He had invited me to a walk on the beach early that morning, and I loved racing him along the shoreline. We pretended to escape each hot lava wave crawling up the sand. After we had played our game, Dad picked me up and said, "Let's go into the ocean!" I did not like his suggestion. The vastness of the water frightened me, and I wanted to keep playing games on the shore. But it was too late; I was scooped up in his arms. I kicked and screamed. He smiled and giggled a little bit, while my four-year-old, fearful heart overflowed, "No! No!" My dad was calm and full of joy. He kept walking toward the water. I felt the waves graze my toes and I screamed even louder, my body stiff as a board in his gentle arms. He kept walking into the sea until we both were fully immersed in the water. I became quiet. He was still smiling. My emotions swung like a pendulum, and I suddenly broke out into laughter. I loved the water, and he knew I would.

My dad did not put me down on the sand, look me in the eyes and explain his reasoning for taking me into the ocean. He didn't try to convince me I was going to love the water. He was smarter than that. My dad saw me flailing, full of fear and didn't mock me with his smile. He was smiling because he knew my fear needed to be conquered while I was wrapped up in his safe arms. My dad grew up loving the water. He has his own memories of his father taking him into the ocean and doing somersaults in the rolling waves. My dad wanted to create a moment with me to enjoy the gift his father gave to him. He wanted to have fun with me. In my child's mind, I thought the two of us were just going on a walk, but my dad was thinking about something much bigger. He wanted to give me a gift.

My dad empathized with me. Empathy is the feeling of understanding and sharing another person's experiences and emotions (Merriam-Webster). In that moment, my dad knew how afraid I was, but he didn't feel sorry for me. He saw my fear and knew that the best thing—the most healing thing—would be to go directly to the water. If my dad had sympathized with me (the feeling of being sorry about someone else's trouble, grief, misfortune), we would never have gotten in the water. My dad didn't give fear the right to sculpt my opinion about the ocean—not when he knew the beauty, joy and adventure it offered.

God can take our "yes" and teach us about His nature; He takes us much further than we feel we are capable. God carries our burdens with us, and His heart breaks for us when we are in pain, but He does not feel sorry for us. He is not a sympathizing God; He is an empathizing God. He won't let go, and He won't react to our fearful outbursts. Jesus came and lived a human life not to feel sorry for us, but to understand every moment we walk through and to get every key we need. He came so that we could have a constant connection with the Father through His Spirit.

Prompt: Are there places in your heart that you've wanted God to give up and feel sorry for you? Are there places where you've seen a passive God who won't use your "yes" to heal your heart from fear? Pull out your journal and write a prayer to the Father; repent for viewing Him as a weak, controllable God. Then, dare to record His response. Don't be afraid!

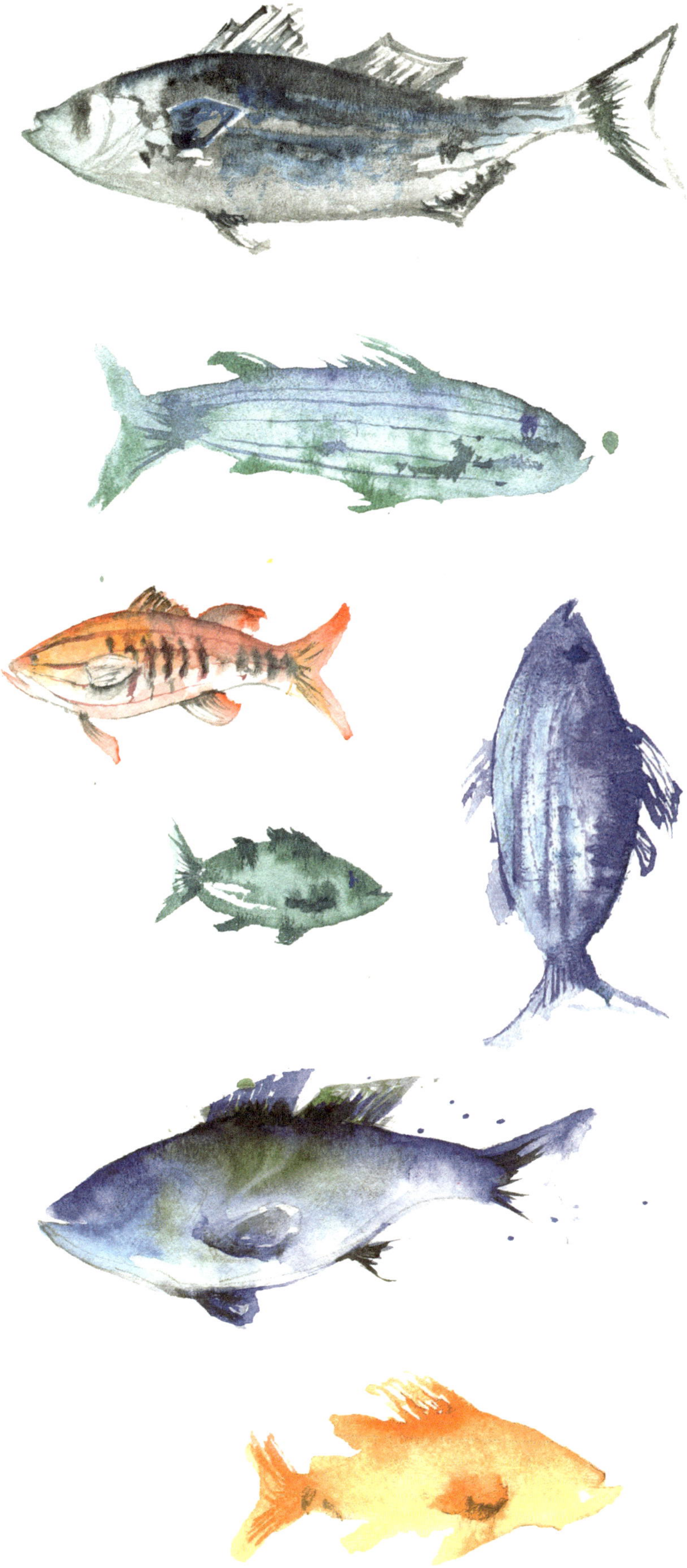

№ 15

FEEDING THE FIVE THOUSAND

RECIPE FOR READING GOD'S WORD / BY MELISSA HELSER / PAINTING BY LINDSAY VANCE

When Jesus landed and saw a large crowd, he had compassion on them, because they were like sheep without a shepherd. So he began teaching them many things. By this time it was late in the day, so his disciples came to him. "This is a remote place," they said, "and it's already very late. Send the people away so that they can go to the surrounding countryside and villages and buy themselves something to eat." But he answered, "You give them something to eat."... Then Jesus directed them to have all the people sit down in groups on the green grass. So they sat down in groups of hundreds and fifties. Taking the five loaves and the two fish and looking up to heaven, he gave thanks and broke the loaves. Then he gave them to his disciples to distribute to the people. He also divided the two fish among them all. They all ate and were satisfied, and the disciples picked up twelve basketfuls of broken pieces of bread and fish. The number of the men who had eaten was five thousand.
(Mark 6:34-44, NIV)

There are so many facets of relationship. Exhaustion, hunger, impossibility, testing, faith, joy and then wonder and the miraculous. As I grow in life and in my relationship with the Lord, I read the Bible completely differently. I have become more fascinated with the humanity of the Word and the hope it gives us as humans to live a life of radical love and adventure. If you stop and approach the word of God with a heart of wonder and understanding, you will find a story that is beyond anything we could make up. Jesus was always moved by the true nature of His Father in Heaven. He was moved with compassion for the people—not duty or striving or a need to prove Himself to His peers and His followers. He was so connected and rooted in His internal space that when He came to a moment of impossibility, it had to bow to the strength of His interior life. His interior life had consisted of thirty years of patient growth in His understanding of the love of a Father. His ministry was marked with the delight of the Father's pleasure and smile. "This is my son, whom I love; with him I am well pleased" (Matthew 3:17, NIV)

When I sit and imagine the moment of Jesus and His boys surrounded by thousands and thousands of people, I have a tendency to become overwhelmed with the thought of trying to fix that situation. I am learning to establish my inner life in the confidence of who God is and what He wants to be for us. When I discipline myself to look beyond anxiety, I see the faces of the disciples watching the five loaves and two fish transform into an endless supply of provision. I see them looking back at Jesus laughing, with eyes of wonder and astonishment. I love to get lost in the idea that Jesus did this miracle not only to feed the thousands, but to inspire and fill His disciples with faith and joy. He did it to remind them that they serve a God who meets every need. I love thinking about the family that got the 2,000th piece of bread. They might not have known fully what was happening, but the disciples did. Every reach into the basket was building wonder and trust.

We must not take out of these stories the wonder and childlike faith that are the cornerstones of our faith. It is vital to the health of our "fly high" moments that we ask ourselves, *Who is this for?* We must have the patience and the awareness to stop and look beyond the obvious. Don't you love that there were so many layers to this miracle? Jesus had the ability to see the multitudes and the ones He was leading and somehow maintain His inner world of friendship with the Father. If we don't give our hearts to remembering the beauty of how Jesus facilitated these moments, we miss the lesson of simplicity and the need for relationship. Jesus was consistently demonstrating His love for humanity. Intertwined in this crescendo of the miraculous was a golden thread of the nature and intent of the God we serve. I believe that this miracle was as much for the friends of Jesus as it was for the thousands. It was as much about their journey of believing in Jesus as it was the corporate moment.

The way Jesus did ministry has compelled Jonathan and I to build ministry and life with people who we trust, to nurture and cultivate all of the in between, mundane life moments as well as the ones when the whole world is watching us. I can only imagine the conversation around the fire that happened when Jesus and His boys talked about that moment. I smile big and am filled with thankfulness that we serve a God who cares about friendship.

Prompt: Take a moment to read this story from Mark again. Read it through a lens of friendship. Imagine you are one of His disciples. Put yourself in the position of handing out the bread and fish. Look back at Jesus and see His smile. Ask Him to fill your heart with His desire to love and provide for His kids. Ask Him to let you become astonished again with the stories that seem so familiar.

N⁰. 16

TYING LOOSE ENDS

RECIPE FOR COMMITMENT / BY KATELAND CASE

In the winter of 2010, I was in the thick of raising support for missions. I was working two jobs and taking custom crochet orders on the side, and I had a thought. Why not have a house show to sell my handmade goods? It would be so easy! In my enthusiasm to get things going, I began several projects. I would see something that inspired me and go to the store to pick out a special skein of yarn. Then suddenly, while working on the piece, I'd think up another amazing idea and abandon the one I'd been working on. Full of inspiration, I'd rush back to the store to choose supplies for this newer idea. I remember my sister standing with me in the fibers aisle of a craft store and insisting, "Kateland! You cannot buy any more yarn! You have so much already—you already have everything you need." Frustrated, I ignored her and bought the skeins I was so sure I needed to fulfill my latest idea. I stayed in a state of being so inspired that I found myself not finishing any projects. I was in chronic "open mode," and didn't see one concept through to completion. My floor was covered in bursts of orange and blue, in gray and white patterns, with tassels and yarn scraps everywhere.

A week before my show I realized just what I had set myself up for. Although I had dozens of pieces well under way, not a single one was completed. They were lacking in embellishments, they hadn't been tied off, and some were in very early stages. Anxious and totally overwhelmed, I sat on my floor feeling like I was drowning in yarn and my inability to commit. Then I felt the presence of the Father rest next to me on my crochet-covered floor. I heard Him say, "Kateland, I want to teach you to finish projects." I looked at all the piles of yarn around me, and I realized that these pieces I began were not just crochet projects. They represented piles of unfinished, uncommitted places in my heart with the Father. Places I didn't follow through.

"Character is walking out a commitment once the emotion is gone." - Ken Helser

It was there on my bedroom floor, in the midst of uncompleted commitments, that I had a collision with my lack of character. There were so many willing and eager places in my heart where I had said yes to Jesus. But as soon as the excitement of this new revelation wore off, my heart would eagerly begin searching for the next big moment—the next sign that He knew what my heart needed. My lack of finishing projects was actually affecting my love for crochet. This idea didn't only apply to my craft. Because I wasn't carrying out the commitments to Jesus I had made in my heart, I felt my delight in our relationship fading. I was disconnected, overstimulated and unaware of what I had the capacity to handle.

But He was excited to step in and help me see things through to completion. It was there, right before my house show that He and I began a journey of finishing. Practically, at that specific point, I had to pull all-nighters to fulfill my commitment to the house show, which wasn't ideal. However, that scenario marked my heart to be a woman of character, a person who sets herself up for success in keeping the commitments she makes.

It is so easy to lose focus, to become inspired by other people, to become overwhelmed by all the things we want to change and do and become. Our struggle as a generation is that we are constantly getting inspired, but rarely do we follow through with our inspirations. I believe that the Father wants to sit beside us in the midst of all of our ideas and ambitions and teach us how to see things through to completion. He wants to meet us in the follow through.

Prompt: Close your eyes and invite the Holy Spirit to remind you of a project you haven't finished. Is it a painting you began? A card you started writing to a friend? Fixing the pipe under the kitchen sink? Whatever it is, thank the Father for bringing it back to your memory. Set some time aside to work on this specific thing. As you set your hands to it again, ask the Father to teach you something about completion. Ask Him, "Father, where is an area in my life that you are inviting me to follow through? How do you want to teach me to commit?" Enjoy your conversation with Him as you finish a practical task, and reflect on your conversation in your journal when you're finished.

LIVING FROM BLESSING

RECIPE FOR CRAFTED PRAYER / BY JOEL CASE

God does not micromanage our lives. He doesn't cling to us and control us. He isn't a backseat driver, smothering us with reminders and worrying the whole way. No. God releases us. "Be fruitful and multiply and fill the earth and subdue it" (Genesis 1:28, ESV). That blessing is enough to lead and guide us, even when we don't see His hand leading us. It is so powerful to discover God's leadership and presence in His permission in our lives.

Twelve years ago, I was trying to decide what I wanted to do after I graduated from high school. I had a few colleges in mind, several of which I had visited. But when the time came to make a decision, I didn't know what to do. It got really complicated in my mind. I didn't have a word from the Lord or any strong sense of direction. All I remembered was that when I first saw an ad for the college that I ended up attending, I felt a sense of peace and excitement inside. So I decided to move halfway across the country to attend. God invaded my life that first semester in ways that only He can take credit for orchestrating. My inner world was profoundly transformed, and the course of my life turned like a large door on the small hinges of chance and risk. I was profoundly impacted by the reality of God's sovereignty and His ability to lead me without controlling me. I felt surrounded and covered, supported and seen by God. I felt so free to run and play in the story God was writing for me. That experience changed everything.

I used to fast and beg for signs and answers to externally come to me when making decisions. Reflecting back now, I think it was because I didn't trust myself. I didn't think I was supposed to. I had picked up a sort of self-hatred, a belief that God's children were internally unreliable with deceitfully wicked hearts. And that's how I saw myself. Punished. Love withheld. I was a slave, not a son. I didn't know that God liked me and actually enjoyed being around me! In His kindness, God never came to me in the way I was seeking. He never wanted to affirm these distorted beliefs I had in my heart. If He had written it on the wall, I could be sure I would please Him and pick the right thing. But if He wrote it on my heart, I had to take a chance and trust. And trust was what He was after. God was teaching me about His all-encompassing love for me. He was eradicating the fear of failure, the fear of rejection, the fear of punishment and the fear of exposure. I couldn't fail with such love in my life.

Many lies keep us from living as beloved sons and daughters: "You're not good enough. You haven't done enough. It wasn't right enough. You missed it. You'll never get it back." Our confidence in our connection with God can weaken under the weight of such lies. But the truth is we are blessed before we set out to do anything. We are enough. We are righteous, beloved children of a loving Father. We are loved by God before we love Him (see I John 4:19). Every initiation on our part exists in response to a greater initiation by God.

Prompt: Journal God's response to this question: Father, how do you want to upgrade the way I have been seeing my life with you? Show me the places I have been afraid to trust you, and myself, to follow the compass you placed inside me as your child when you blessed me. Speak to me, and untether me from fear now in Jesus' name.

NO. 18

STEWARDING GOD'S GIFTS

RECIPE FOR DISCIPLINE
WRITING AND PAINTING BY CADENCE ZION HELSER
AGE 14

My favorite thing to do is play piano. Ever since I was little, I have always wanted to play an instrument like my parents. When I was really young, I used to sit beside my dad on the piano bench while he would play and I would try to play along with him. These moments sparked a love for music in my heart.

Over the past few years, God has been teaching me how to be persistent and disciplined in the things I do and love. Every time I sit down at the piano with my teacher, Molly, or learn to paint with my grandpa, I am humbled by the legacy and knowledge that they carry and are willing to share with me. I am realizing that God wants to freely give me His wisdom just like all of the people in my life do. This truth is encouraging me to ask Him for the things that He is willing to give. It is also challenging me to enjoy the process and the time it takes to create the thing I am asking for.

Prompt: What is your favorite thing to do? Have you realized that God has so much wisdom to give you in the thing you love? Next time you do it, look for God there.

NO. 19

THE BALANCE

RECIPE FOR SONSHIP / BY JAKE STEVENS / PHOTO BY MORGAN CAMPBELL

There are times when I feel like I live in two worlds. The first world is full of sound and creativity. Full of dreaming and fighting for the songs in my friends' hearts. Full of traveling, schedules and meeting new people. Full of worship moments where we as a band feel like we're floating in the presence of God.

The other world is full of practical manual labor, full of caring for fifty-two acres. Mowing grass and fixing sinks. Making phone calls to lumberjacks, electricians, plumbers and contractors. A world of teaching young men in our discipleship schools how to use their hands and take pride in hard work.

Both worlds require my two hands and both worlds have required two different things of me. They have shaped my character and my understanding of the Father's heart.

Eight years ago when I drove onto the property of A Place for the Heart, I had no idea that I could care for a piece of land so deeply. On this land I have been initiated by my leaders, Ken and Jonathan Helser. They have taught me to use a chainsaw, drive a tractor, wire a building. But most importantly, they've taught me ownership. The amazing part of working for this ministry is that all of our tools—every saw, every screwdriver—have been bought with money provided by supporters, people who are making sacrifices to support our ministry. One thing I've realized is that many young adults don't actually know how to fight for or appreciate something unless they pay for it themselves. My job requires caring for hundreds of things that I didn't have to pay for and learning how to value the sacrifices of other people. Yet one of the greatest revelations I've had during my time at the farm is that my honor for every drill and every shovel is vitally important. It is important because I am taking ownership of something I didn't have to pay for, treating it as my own and setting a value system for those around me. This is how Jesus gives to us. Total access to priceless items, yet how often do we actually realize the value in what He's given? How many times do we have to break something valuable before we understand its value? These are lessons I am still learning.

Eight years ago, I simultaneously began another journey. It all began when Jonathan and Melissa took a risk one Friday night at a local church and asked me to play electric guitar for them. It was a trial run; they had never heard me play, and I was pretty dang nervous. The presence of the Lord showed up that night, and a beautiful connection between the Helsers and I began to take root. A sound within me came alive while I played their music, and a sound was released in them as I stood behind them and supported their sound. Since then we've gone on countless trips. We've engaged glorious moments in worship where God has touched Earth through the songs they've sung and the melodies I've played. In teaming with Jonathan and Melissa's sound, I have learned more about unity in the Spirit and consistent sensitivity to where the Father is leading us. It has required a patience in my heart to stay engaged and has awakened a deep creativity within me.

Recently I went to record with Jonathan and Melissa in Nashville, and there were so many moments when I locked eyes with them and we all smiled because the melodies coming out of my fingers uniquely fit the songs they wrote. It was in this moment that I realized that the reward for consistency and serving my leaders' sound is deep confidence and effortless creativity.

Both sides of my job have pushed me to fly high and build home. These two worlds, although they sometimes seem like they're pulling me in two different directions, have become an anchor for my soul and feed two different desires that God put in my heart. Both parts of my job have become a catalyst for my maturity in the Lord. There are places where the Father has met me in my pursuit of music where I couldn't be met in the practical, hands-on work of the farm. And there are places where God has fathered me in the midst of my hard work on the land that I would have missed on a stage. I am learning to thrive in this balance and the fruit of giving into it has produced character in my life.

Prompt: Make a list of the places that are currently stretching you. Then, ask the Father these questions: "God, how do you want to marry the seemingly unrelated worlds I am living in? Where do you want to grow character in my everyday life?"

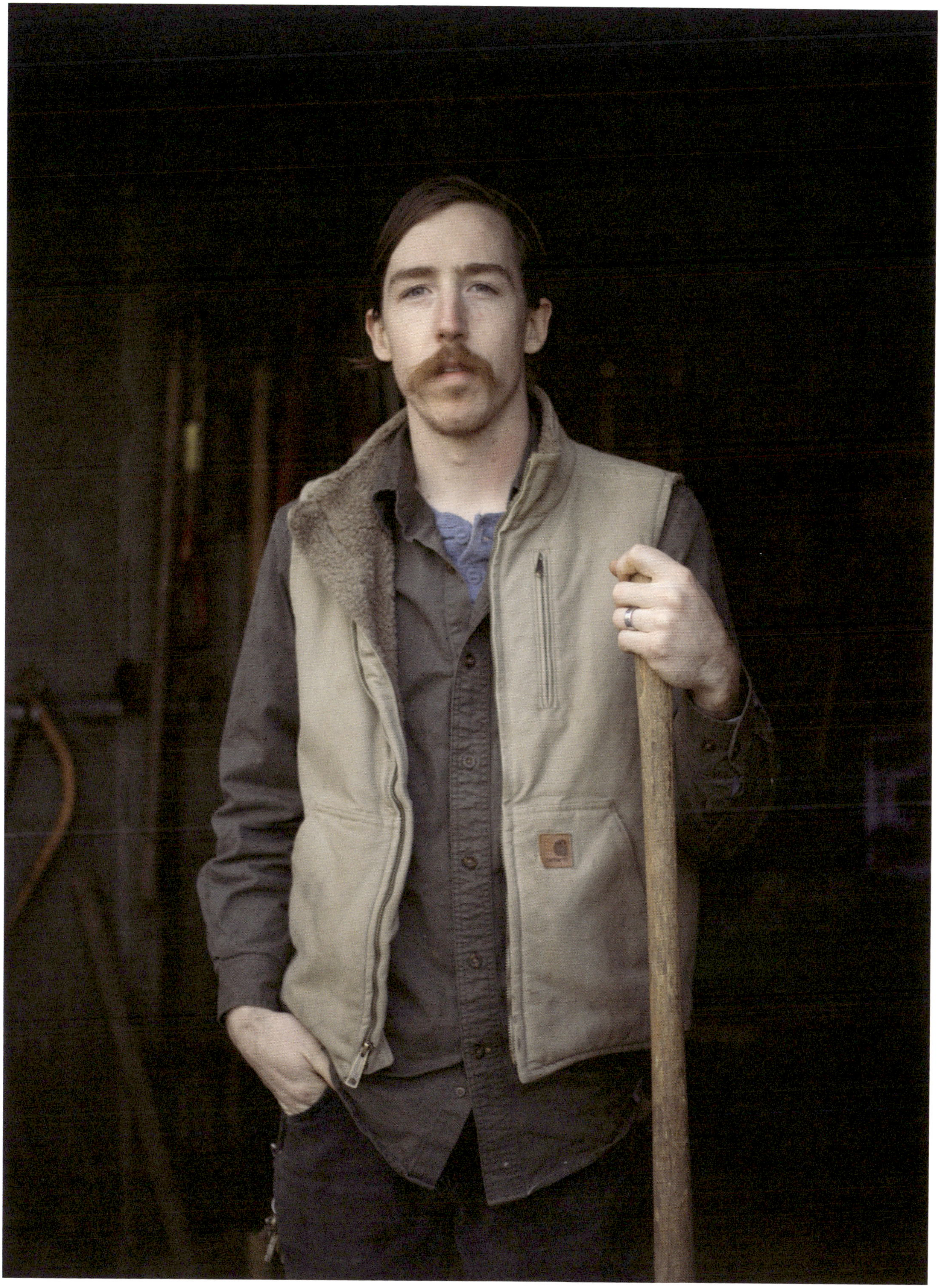

MACARONS

RECIPE FOR INVITING GOD'S VOICE / BY MARTHA MCRAE

When I was child I fell in love with baking in the kitchen. I would watch my mother make biscuits with the toss of flour in the air and the rolling out of the dough. I loved getting my hands messy. As an adult, my delight in baking has not changed. The desire to become a pastry chef was one of my deepest dreams through my young adulthood. Three years ago the Father met me in this deep desire.

That year, my friend Dustie approached me with her idea of creating a one-of-a-kind restaurant in Asheboro, North Carolina called The Table. Her dream was to have a high-quality bakery, offering pastries, savory meals and delicious coffee. In her dream, she imagined me, apron on, kneading dough in the back of the store. My heart flooded with joy. In someone's vision for her restaurant, she pictured me there working, doing the exact job I've always wanted. What a gift from the Father!

I remember my first months of working at The Table when I began to dream into what I wanted to specialize in. There were three pastry chefs at the shop. The ladies I was working with all had their realm of expertise, and I was ready to find mine. One French pastry that I always admired but had never ventured into was French Macarons. The bright, airy, sweet, saucer-shaped delicacy. I found myself dreaming at night about them. I was going to master them. I could feel it. My boss gave me two months to learn and refine the project.

My first attempt to create macarons was nothing short of a complete fail. I took all my knowledge of crusts, cakes and fillings and and tried to apply it to my first venture in creating this unique pastry, but I should have left all my knowledge behind me. Macarons would require a brand new set of rules and understanding. As I worked my way through batch after batch, I adjusted my egg white and almond flour, attempting to find the perfect balance of air and density in the cap. Almost two months in and countless batches later, I still didn't have a successful batch. Each round of macarons would almost work, the caps would look perfect, and then crack. They would turn out lopsided because there was too much sugar. The cap wouldn't rise so there would be no air. I was frustrated. I sat and problem-solved so many times.

Two days before my deadline, I walked into the store. I knew that I had to figure it out that day. I sat at the counter. There are only four ingredients in a macaron. On paper it's uncomplicated, but in the science of baking, it has to be perfectly balanced for the pastry to fill with air and still be crisp. I invited the Holy Spirit into the process and asked Him, "Will you show me how to do this?" I felt Him whisper to me, "You should adjust the egg whites—add more." His voice was the only idea in my head. I listened. I adjusted my ratio one more time.

I was nervous. I was in the middle of a deadline. Would it work?

Hours later, I opened the heavy oven door to reveal a batch of perfectly balanced macarons. I was undone. The Creator of the universe just fit Himself inside our little bakery to show me the secret of making a perfect macaron! I was humbled, excited and relieved. The Holy Spirit came, and I met my deadline.

Prompt: This moment changed my life because I realized that the Father wanted me to succeed and meet my deadline even more than I did. It was His greatest desire to fit Himself inside of that tiny bakery—to meet me where I was and help me problem-solve. Ask the Father to reveal a place where you are leaving Him out of your ordinary day. Pray: "Father, where is a place I amnot leaving room for you to come in? How do you want to fit yourself inside of my mundane to meet me and help me succeed?" Let your heart be encouraged as you journal His response.

POPPY SEED *to* LEMON

BY ERIN GRAVITT

The first part of this poem was written when my daughter was the size of a tiny poppy seed inside of my womb. My husband and I had just discovered we were pregnant, and I was filled with a panic of the unknown and a gaping denial. Through countless prayers, the devotion and peace of my husband, the lifting-up from friends and family and the eminent grace of God, I had the valiant joy to write the second part of this poem ten weeks later. The fog of discomfort and selfishness cleared as I remembered the life-giving, rewarding promises of the Lord and actually believed them.

Part I

You live in darkness, clothed in black,
I cannot see you, smell you, feel you,
yet you are there, I think, who knows.
Utter seclusion, you frighten me,
so minuscule, and I, grown and
powerful, this I thought, but now
denial ever-present, perhaps you
have more strength than I realize.

What I know to be true is that all
things have a way of working out,
though now, a looming danger,
death of self waiting, not ready,
not now, it can't be, what I do not
behold is not, yes or no,
real or imaginary, even a sure thing
doesn't necessarily bring peace,
God, only You know, only resort.

Part II

Life is lighter now that we know,
he knows, she knows, they know,
celebration and a sigh of relief on
the other side of time, settling,
thinking, praying, sharing.
Clarity comes with remembrance
of promise, and Your word
brings ease to the heavy load.

No longer a secret, though still
being made there, I wonder
what you look like and who you
will be, alive and living,
forming and functioning.
You change everything,
God, You give heritage and reward.

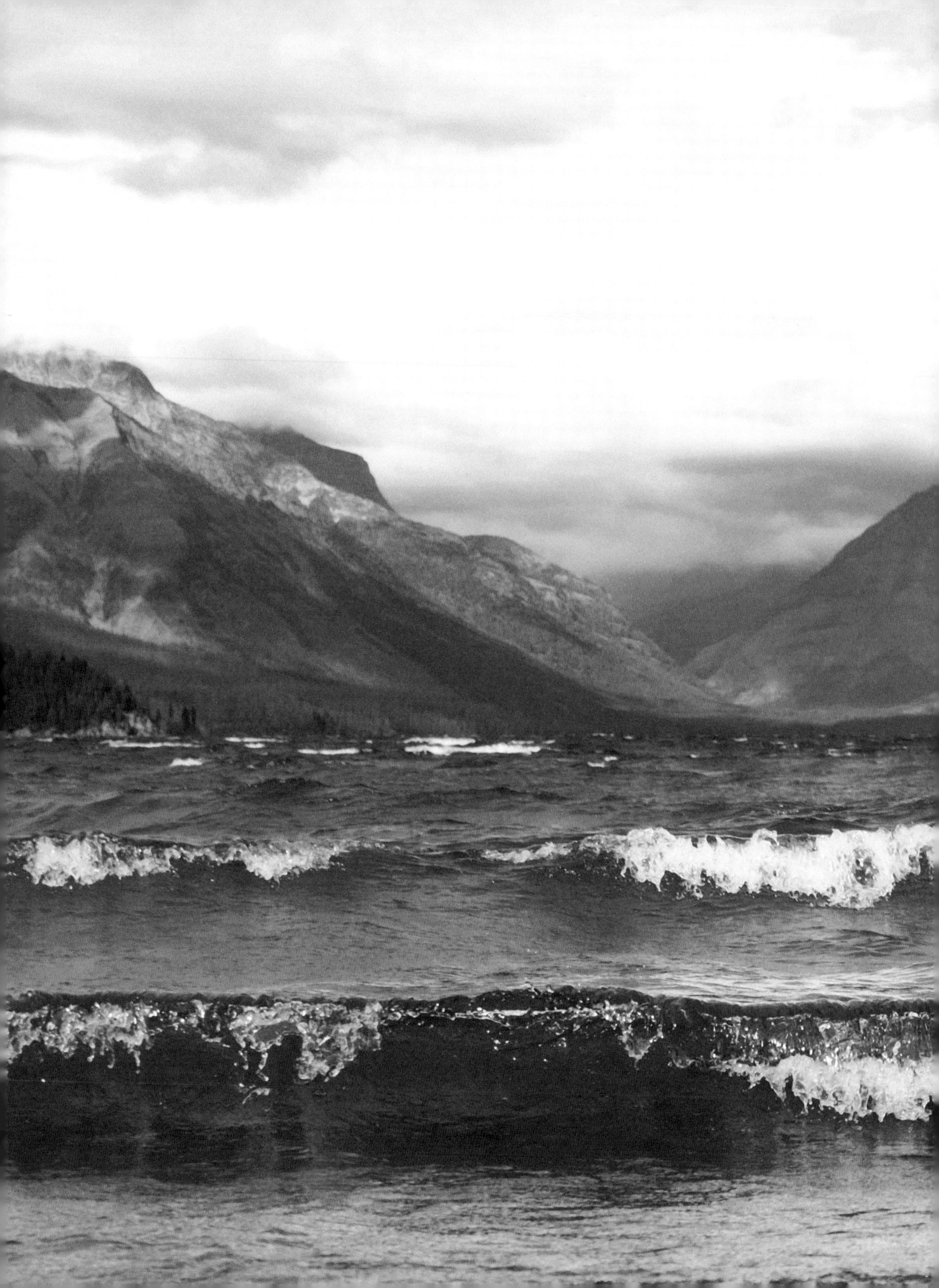

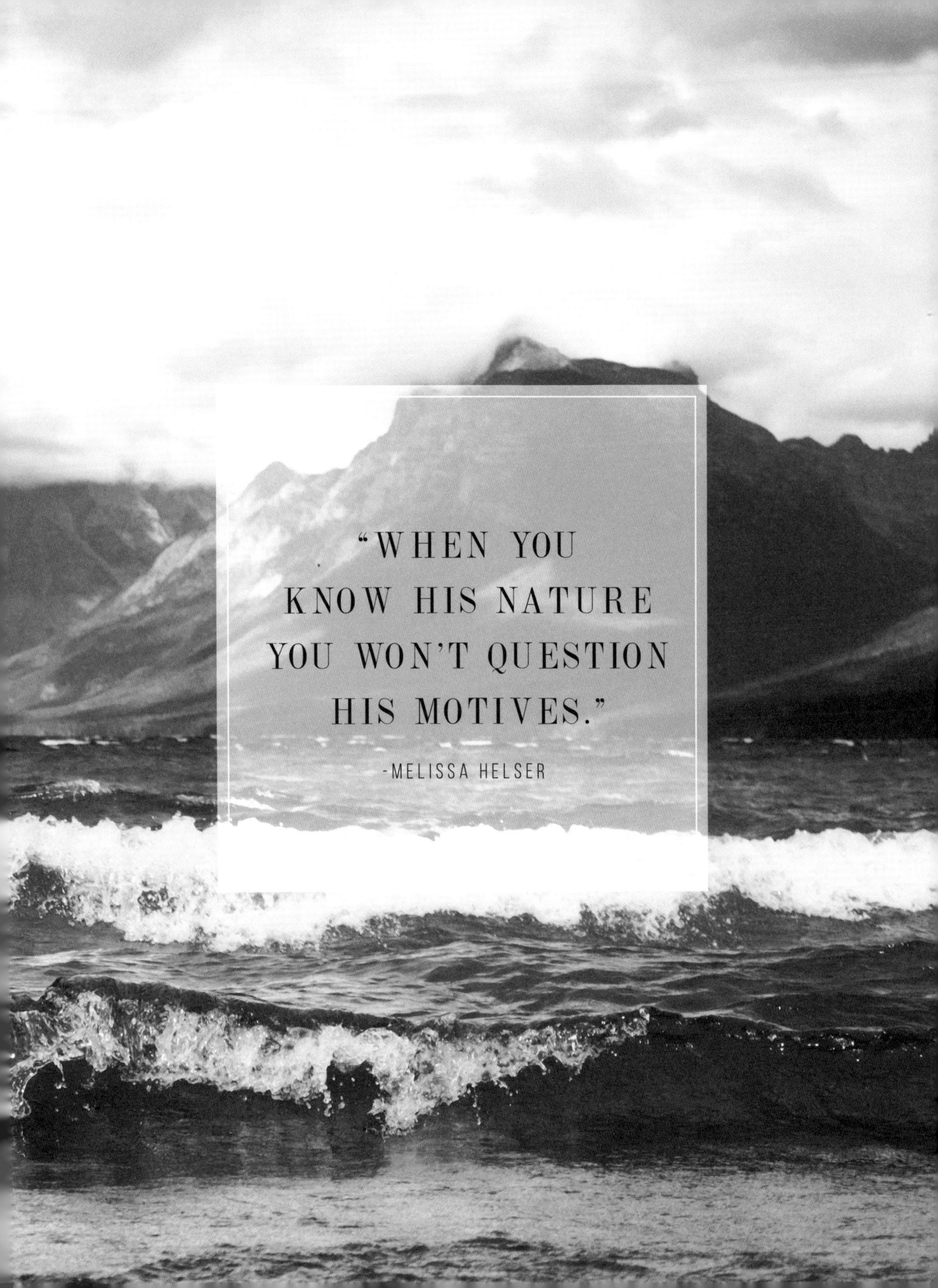

"WHEN YOU KNOW HIS NATURE YOU WON'T QUESTION HIS MOTIVES."

-MELISSA HELSER

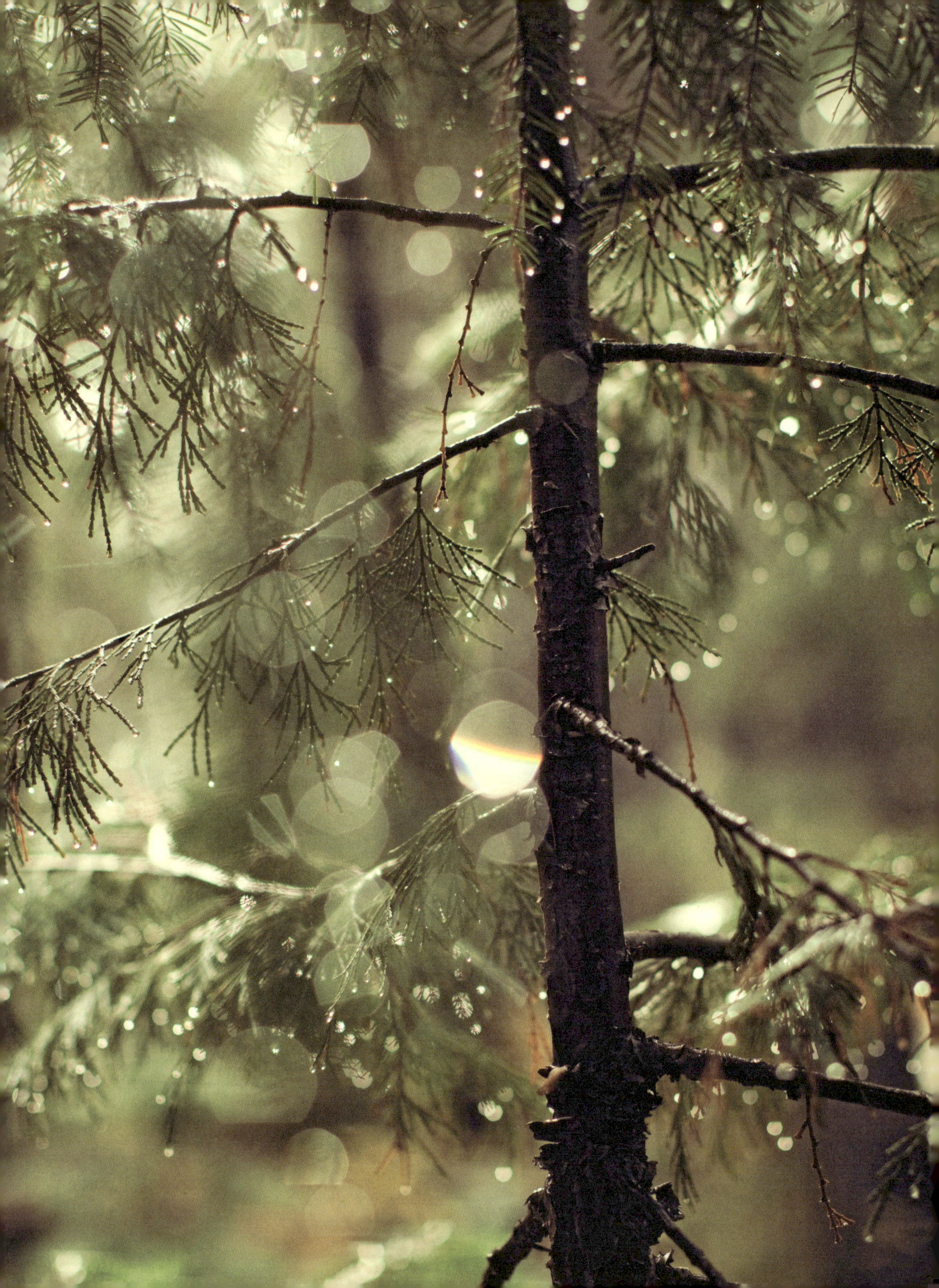

WHO TENDS THE FOREST

BY EMILY PELL / PHOTO BY GINNY CORBETT

Who tends the far-reaching forest?
Who prepares the soil, breathing life into the depths?
Who stoops low to plant the mighty oaks and poplars?
Who shows the maple where to stand?
Who walks among the saplings
encouraging them to embrace both wind and storm?
Who sings songs of love to the oak
causing it to never weary of dancing in the sun?
Who wraps the forest with light
and covers it when darkness closes in?
Who celebrates each bud in spring
and each fire-touched leaf in autumn?
Who tends the forest?

"I can tend the land," I say.
I toil over my small plot.
I swing the hoe with haste and call the soil prepared.
I plant each seedling in the thick rocky soil where I think
it should go.
I try to water each seed that it might grow.
With hard labor and the sweat of my brow
I strive to tend what is mine.
But even in all my labor, I cannot make it grow.

I set my shovel down and step into
Something greater than me.
I longingly ask the forest, "Who tends you?"
I look at the small sapling craving to know who prepared
the soil and watered the seed.
I watch the leaves unfold and know that the One who
tends is much bigger than me.
I gaze at the mighty oak and faintly hear oak's love song
lifting on the breeze.
I call on the Wind, "Come tend me!"

from the GARDEN

WRITING AND PAINTINGS BY
LINDSAY VANCE

Recently I heard God say, "Lindsay, you are approaching spending time with me as if you are making a trip to the drive-thru, asking for fried food that has been picked over and left out, prepared by a chef who had no thought of you in mind." As God began speaking, I realized I had a fear that the Lord was not preparing anything special for me in my quiet times; therefore, I had taught my heart to expect stale, cheap and mass-produced food from God. It's a funny analogy, but it's true. Upon addressing my unbelief, God began to reveal what He was truly preparing for me each time I drew close to Him.

MY FEAR CRUMBLED UNDER THE REVELATION THAT THE LORD HANDPICKS AND HANDCRAFTS A MEAL FOR ME EVERY TIME I MEET WITH HIM.

He gives me food for my soul that is straight from His garden—seasonal fruits and vegetables that are appropriate and timely to complement the season of my life. God doesn't just feed me—He delights in nourishing me.

God longs to feed our hearts with His word (the Bible) and the Word (Jesus). He knows what we need. He has considered the rich colors that will energize our spirits. He knows what we like—the foods that will make us exclaim, "God, you know and love me so well!" He is a creative God who gave us a hunger for natural foods so we can better understand our deep hunger for Him. He is the Bread of Life, and He is feeding us from His hand everyday.

This series, From the Garden, is a group of prompts meant to engage your imagination and inspire you to believe that God is serving you custom-made, handcrafted meals for your heart. He is not a drive-thru God. He is the Gardener who died to feed you everything that the Cross affords.

1.
SEASON

"There is a time for everything, and a season for every activity under the heavens" (Ecclesiastes 3:1, NIV).

I am convinced that the ripe, red sweetness of a summer watermelon is one of the best flavors on Earth. In the hot months of July and August, I relish the juicy fruit overflowing from each bite, spilling down the sides of my mouth and coating my hands with sticky sweetness. I love how eating watermelon makes me feel like a kid again. Against the blazing sun—coolness, energy, relief. It is unlikely that we would freeze watermelon to save for the cooler months, and we certainly don't can it to eat when winter comes; but we do await the sweetness for a whole year to savor what can be harvested in just a few weekends.

God designed the fruit of our lives to be harvested in seasons. We were not meant to be satisfied by watermelon throughout the year. Its juicy goodness would not satisfy our need for hearty foods that we crave in darker months. As the days begin to shorten and the heat gives way to autumn, we make space in our hearts for the fruit of another season, earthier garden vegetables that nourish different parts of our souls.

Prompt: What God chose to feed you in the past may not nourish your heart like it once did. Are there places where you have desired that the Lord give you exactly what He gave in previous seasons? In your journal, make a list of the fruits the Father nourished your heart with in seasons past. Practice remembering God's faithfulness in your story. Just like watermelon running down your chin, remember how God met you with sweetness. Thank Him for His desire to satisfy you and repent for the ways you demanded He come through for you like He has in the past.

Now, with the Holy Spirit, make a list of the fruits God is giving you in this season. Ask the Lord what seasonal fruit He is harvesting in the garden of your heart. What is He inviting you to taste now? Could it be friendship, belonging, stillness, rest? Journal His voice. And then, "taste and see that He is good" (Psalm 34:8, NIV)

2.
BITTER

"No discipline seems pleasant at the time, but painful. Later on however, it produces a harvest of righteousness and peace for those that have been trained by it" (Hebrews 12:11, NIV).

We do not naturally love every good food that God has made. Some foods land on our palate and taste bitter or earthy. Most children do not inherently ask their parents for kale or radishes, but rather their parents must teach them the value of eating such foods. And as we mature, we learn to cultivate a taste for these kinds of bitter fruits because we know they are good for us. We know that they give life to our bodies.

As lovers of God, we can respond in a similar way to the food of the Spirit. I spent a year and a half in the uncomfortable state of constant correction by my leaders. I felt entirely entitled to many things, and God was daily feeding my heart with discipline from my leaders' hands. There were days when I didn't want to give in to their wisdom and submission was really painful. It was hard not to pretend to swallow the bitter fruit only to dishonestly spit it out later. But thank God that I learned not only to swallow the fruit, but also to be thankful for it. I can look back on that season now and see with clear eyes that the Lord was training me. He was developing my taste for discipline. I realized that while correction did not taste particularly sweet on my tongue, if I received it, its benefits would feed my heart. Now, when I am corrected by leaders or by the Lord, I recognize the gift of discipline and know that God wants to grow me. I am living in God's promise of righteousness and peace!

Prompt: Are there places in your heart that have rejected God's discipline? Ask the Lord to help you identify the bitter-tasting fruit of discipline in your life, and then ask Him to help you desire it. Do not be discouraged that you don't like it immediately, but instead craft a thankful prayer to God for His promise of the full harvest of peace and righteousness that is to come. Then journal the Father's voice over you.

3.
WHOLE

"Jesus answered, 'I am the way, the truth and the life'" (John 14:6, NIV).

God is a purist. He feeds us the truest form of the Spirit directly from His hand. God does not offer us processed, watered-down imitations of food that are disguised as natural. His nourishment comes directly from the death and resurrection of Jesus, the One who purifies us and cleanses us from all sin. I love the truth Peter expresses in his second letter to the church: "His divine power has given us everything we need for life and godliness through the full knowledge of the one who called us by his own glory and excellence." (II Peter 1:3, ISV). God has set the table, and He is giving a feast.

Our culture is growing increasingly unable to identify whole foods in their basic form. In this same way, we don't recognize basic truths from God's word. We are used to eating flavored potato chips instead of real potatoes. The enemy wants us to believe that God can be broken down and sectioned out, that we can enjoy Him in the ways we want to enjoy Him, but not take in His fullness. God wants to give us His whole self. He wants to teach us how to detect falsehood from the truth and build up an appetite that craves the whole truth about Him.

Prompt: Read II Peter 1:3 again. Imagine you are sitting at a table God has delightfully set for you. What are some of the foods you see there? Ask the Father what whole spiritual foods He has lovingly prepared for you to feast on. Ask Him to help you detect the false beliefs you have been ingesting. Make an exchange with Him.

"YOU GIVE THEM THEIR FOOD AT THE PROPER TIME. YOU OPEN YOUR HAND AND SATISFY THE DESIRES OF EVERY LIVING THING"

PSALM 145:15-16, NIV

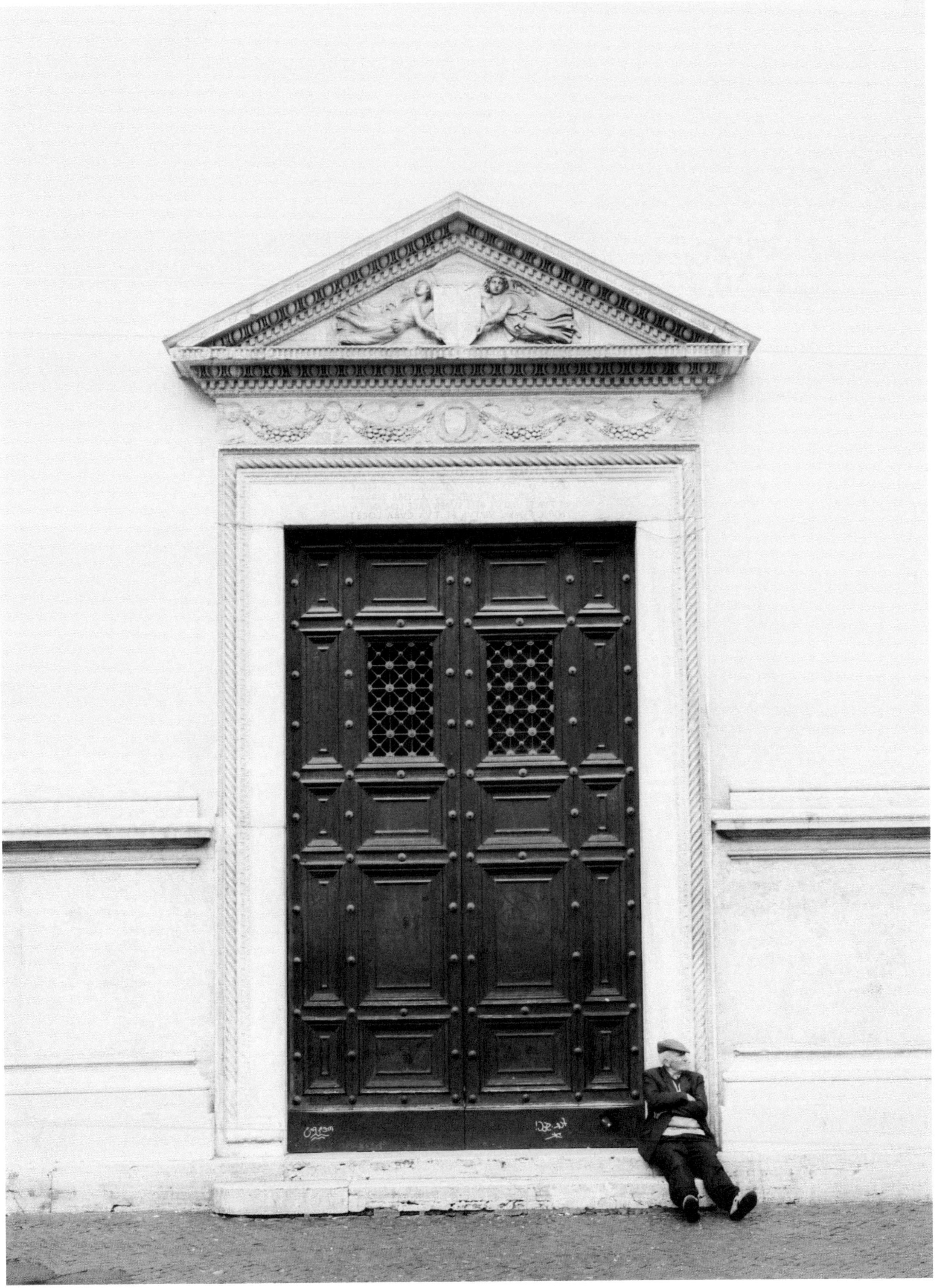

NO. 21

DELIVERY CONFIRMATION

RECIPE FOR THANKSGIVING / BY JONATHAN DAVID HELSER / PHOTO BY GINNY CORBETT

One of the ways I best communicate love is through giving gifts. I once mailed a very special gift to a friend. This package contained a gift that was quite valuable and could not be replaced. I made sure to pay the extra cost for insured tracking at the post office. I even gave them my e-mail address so they could send me a delivery notification once the package was received. I remember checking my e-mail account each day in excited, nervous anticipation to see if the gift had arrived at its destination. It was a thrilling moment when the delivery confirmation came into my inbox. As I read the e-mail, a deep satisfaction filled my heart as the giver. My gift had safely reached my friend.

Prompt: When we stop and acknowledge the gifts the Lord has given us and give thanks for them, we send a delivery notification to Heaven's inbox. Imagine the satisfaction that fills the heart of the Father when He sees that His gifts have reached their intended destination. Gratefulness is like signing your name on the delivery ticket, "This package was meant for me!" Take a moment, and write a list of the gifts you have received from God. With your list, express your thanks for each gift by name and acknowledge that you have received them. Feel the Father's smile and satisfaction.

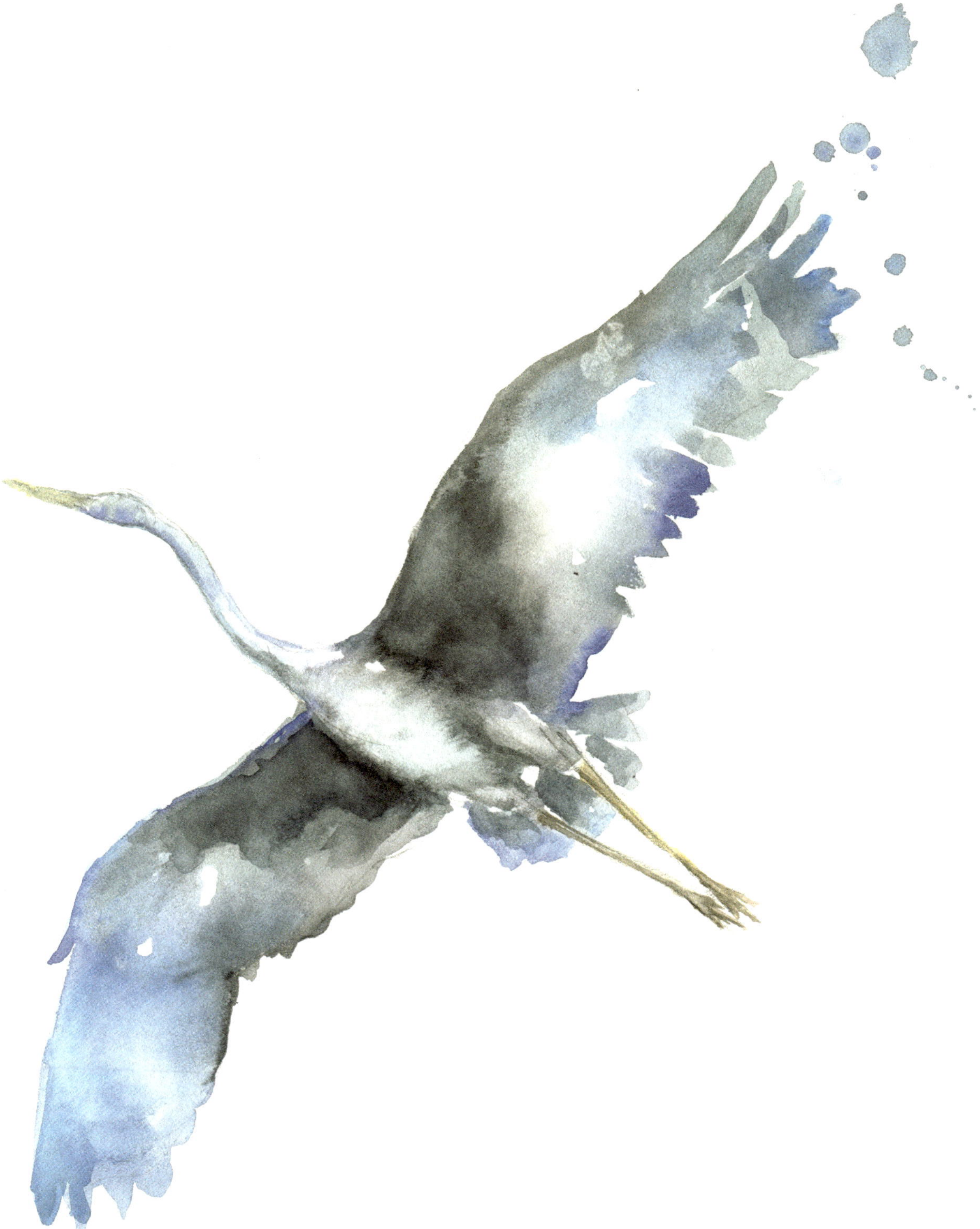

harness the wind

YOU KNOW WELL ENOUGH HOW THE WIND BLOWS THIS WAY AND THAT. YOU HEAR IT RUSTLING THROUGH THE TREES, BUT YOU HAVE NO IDEA WHERE IT COMES FROM OR WHERE IT'S HEADED NEXT. THAT'S THE WAY IT IS WITH EVERYONE 'BORN FROM ABOVE' BY THE WIND OF GOD, THE SPIRIT OF GOD.

JOHN 3:8, MSG

SOMETIMES *the* SKY *is* TOO BRIGHT

BY MELISSA HELSER
PHOTO BY GINNY CORBETT

Sometimes the sky is too bright
for me to tip my head back
and see the top of your glorious branches.
I try.
The sun's brilliance blinds me,
thank goodness I am standing in the middle of a wide stream
In its still waters I can see the Reflection of your growth
I stop.
I don't want to stir the waters.
In quiet deep inhales,
I take in your giant branches.
Your deep Roots have served you well.

I see.
Life everywhere,
the Reflection is as true as the real seeing.
When the glory isn't too bright.
I will look at you again
And breathe you
Fully in.

NO. 22

soaring in remembrance

RECIPE FOR UNDERGOING PRESSURE
BY MOLLY KATE SKAGGS

My heart has been fascinated with flight and all flying things ever since I was a child: lightning bugs in the summer time, a mama bird teaching her little ones how to fly, the taking off of an airplane, and those gigantic, brightly colored hot-air balloons floating high with grace and ease. These things filled me with wonder and delight. Back then, the "why" of flight seemed much easier to understand than the "how". The world was simple, and there was little fear in my heart. My choices weren't based on my own capacity, but they were based on the miracle I saw in a hummingbird's fluttering wings and a hot-air balloon's ability to remain suspended in midair.

I am a bit older now. I am a young woman in my early thirties who has seen a lot of life. My heart has been hit with painful disappointments and beautiful healing. My choices have shifted from being based in wonder, to being based in fear, back to being based in the wonder of God. I am pursuing a lifestyle of knowing myself so that I can truly know my Father in Heaven. I believe that this kind of living requires measures of looking back within moments of our lives. Allowing the Father to show us moments in our lives where we agreed with fear rather than faith is a gift and part of the liberation of our souls as sons and daughters. It is all part of the breakdown before the rebuild, and this is the joy of walking out our salvation with the All-Things-New Creator God.

I can recall my college senior recital that took place in the spring of 2007. I was a young, zealous music student who was going for a degree and double-major in music composition and theory. It was indeed an ambitious degree that required a lot of time and work. My senior recital was meant to be the crowning moment of achievement in my undergraduate education, and all things were flowing fast and rapidly toward that one goal of showing my teachers, family and friends how much I had grown and all that I had learned in those five years of concentrated study. My recital was required to be at least sixty-five percent of original music. It was my moment to shine, to set a table and invite others in to celebrate my growth and deeper love for the gifts I was given. It should have been one of the most joyful moments of my life, even if it was full of tremendous work and effort. Unfortunately, fear was steering my ship, and I was sinking further down into the depths of a deep, dark sea. I remember the emotional breakdowns of a billion tears while in the practice rooms. I recall being so frustrated I wanted to rip up my sheet music and run. I remember moments of being so afraid of failing that I would procrastinate and mismanage my time. I remember crazy, frantic sleepless nights and the all-nighters of grueling work trying to finish projects and complete my original pieces. Mostly, I remember the ugly, fearful words deep within my internal space: "Why did I do this? What was I thinking? This is all too much for me. I cannot do this. My recital is going to be the worst. I am going to disappoint everyone…but mostly, I will be a disappointment to myself." I felt lost, alone and completely exhausted in every sphere of my being.

By the time I stood on the stage in our performing arts center on campus, surrounded by my musician friends who were supporting me by performing my pieces, looking down at my teachers, friends and family in their proud, glistening eyes, I felt my heart in full flight. I remember thinking to myself, "How did I actually get here?!" For I truly did feel as though I were flying upon the winds of joy just as I was created to by my Creator-Father. I remember sitting at the piano, taking a deep breath, striking the first chords of one of my original pieces, and looking up to see His smile at the other end of the piano. Tears came into my eyes. My music was good, but, more importantly, my heart knew that it was good. The little girl's heart caught the winds of Perfect Love that day, and the older young woman now sees that He knew exactly what I needed in order to really fly. Because of that beautiful moment, the little girl of First Innocence is able to take up more room in this heart.

I never want to misinterpret or be afraid of the pressure ever again.

All flying things are actually created to defy gravity. In order for flight to happen, just the right amounts of pressure and resistance must take place both within and outside of the craft. In other words, pressure and resistance aren't necessarily negative components in the equation. They are necessary for lift off and soaring! In this particular moment of looking back, I was able to see that all of the internal pressures of feeling worthless, alone and afraid were working with all the practical external pressures of recital goals and deadlines being met. My heart felt trapped within the pressure. My eyes were shrouded by the darkness of my own agreements with lies about who I was and especially who God was in the midst of pressure. But what I couldn't see was that the presence of the Father Himself was hidden in the internal pressure. He was reaching out into the empty spaces and inflating me with His joy, help, bravery and confidence. He saw what I needed in order to lift off the ground, and He knew what my heart needed to fully soar when the day of my recital actually came. Did I pass all the pressure tests with flying colors? Not a chance. But was I doused in His perfect love and amazing grace? Absolutely.

Prompt: It is important for us to look back on moments where fear nearly took us out and see how the Father came through for us. It is necessary for growth and good heart-health to go back in order to really go forward! Take some time with the Father and ask Him to help you recall a moment where you nearly crumbled under pressure. With your journal and pen ready, ask Him these questions: "Father, how did you meet me in the midst of that pressurized situation? How are you helping me to interpret the current pressure I feel in my life?" Humble your heart to receive His perfect love and journal His voice. Let Him fill you with grace for your past and hope for your future!

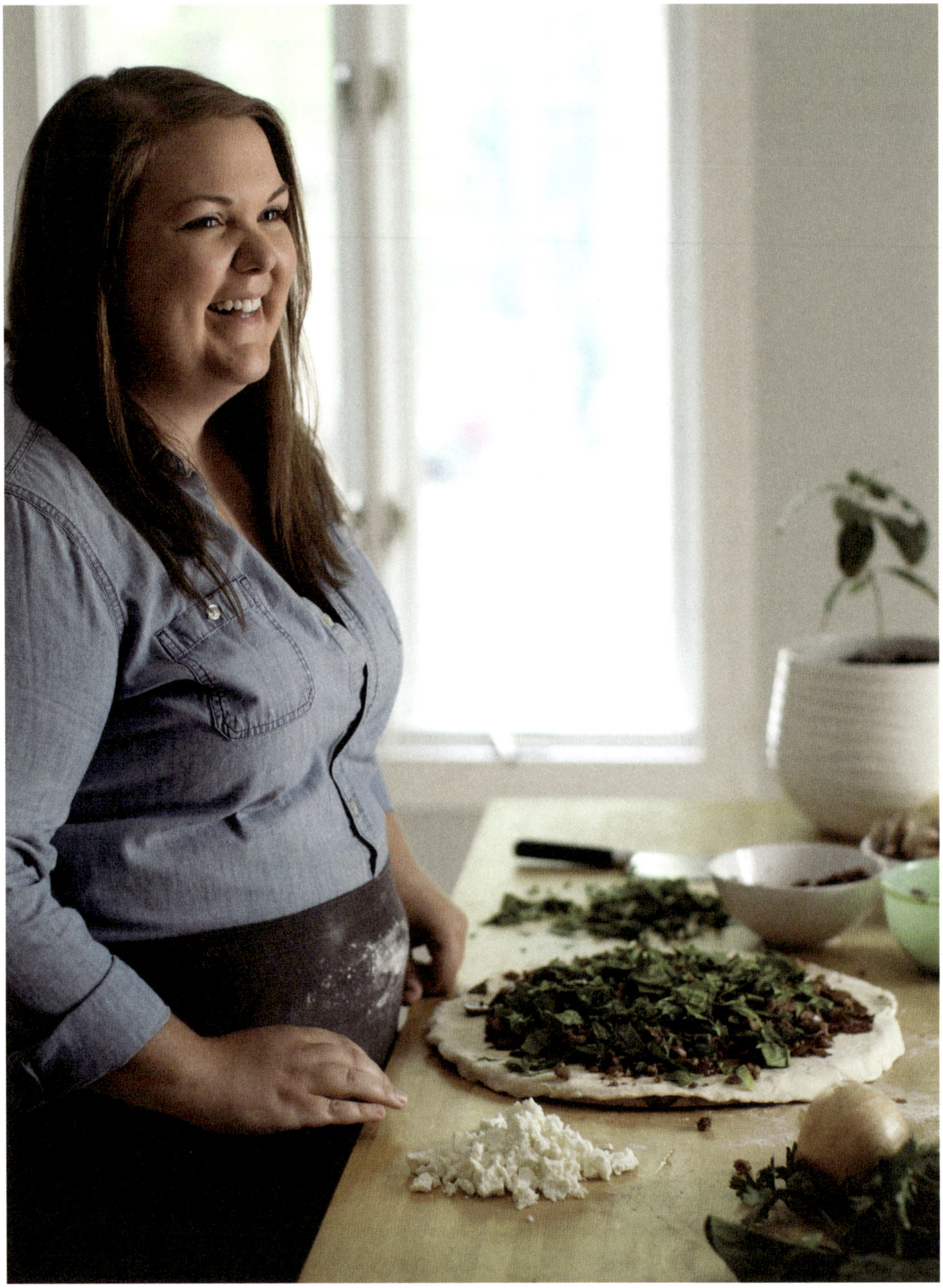

MARTHA'S TABLE

a FEATURE *on* MARTHA MCRAE

WRITTEN BY ALLIE SAMPSON
PHOTOS BY GINNY CORBETT

I often come home to the Farmhouse and am greeted by a decadent aroma. On this particular afternoon I am met with a savory wave of butter, sausage and caramelized onions. A warm light glows from under the closed kitchen door, and a tide of laughter rushes from the room and pulls me in. There is family in the kitchen. I slide the white door aside to find Martha McRae, our Kitchen Manager, behind the island, kneading and working a thick, floury dough. Throughout the room, friends and roommates are crowded around countertops and seated on stools. They are happily recounting the day's events and recalling favorite family memories. I hop up on the edge of the island and ask Martha what she's making. "Rustic tart," she replies with a raise of her eyebrows and a twinkle in her eye. She smiles, knowing it's my favorite, "Would you like some?"

I have encountered Martha in more moments like this than I can count—our community gathered together in the kitchen or at a table for a meal, being seen and known in our friendship and feeling invited into the family. When I first came to the 18 Inch Journey, I was shocked at the homemade quality of the meals. I had assumed we'd eat cheap, mass-produced "camp food"—sloppy joes, hot dogs, frozen french fries and mac 'n cheese. So when dishes like garden-picked kale salad, roasted rosemary chicken, herb-seasoned potatoes and asparagus topped with goat cheese made their way to my plate from Martha's kitchen, I was beyond impressed. Clearly, she had a high value not just for good food, but for the people who would be partaking in it. I was blown away by the devoted effort that went into making me feel welcome. A simple meal communicated to me that I mattered, that I was important, that I was worth extravagance.

The thoughtfulness behind every one of Martha's meals comes from her all-embracing heart and hands. Martha has cultivated a love for preparing quality meals and enjoying them with friends around the table. As the leader of the kitchen at A Place for the Heart, Martha plans and prepares meals for our growing community year-round. She dreams into menu planning, oversees the weekly grocery spree and cooks meals for anywhere between seven and seventy people, depending on our season of discipleship. I have seen her prepare multi-course meals for elaborate functions and considerately serve refreshments for meetings she knows are going to last for hours. Everything Martha sets her hands to is glazed with intentionality.

I recently chatted with Martha over a whimsical dish of sweet potato tacos about her love for preparing a meal and setting a table. She first fell in love with cooking meals for loved ones as a young girl, tending seven acres of North Carolina farmland with her family. "I was always around food and cooking. My parents grew all of our own produce, so the garden was always a family affair. Whether it was harvesting, picking or canning, we were always together. We connected with friends by inviting their families over to help on the farm for the day; then they got to take what they harvested home with them." As for cooking, it was about heritage for her. "I grew up cooking with my mom and two grandmothers. Mealtimes were a real priority. There were very few times my dad didn't come home from work for lunch, and we always had family dinner together. Even if Dad had to go back to work afterward, he always came home for meals; we would wait to eat supper until he was able to join us. I've always associated cooking with family."

Martha's love for gathering friends together for a meal grew in her college years at MorningStar University. "I made it known to my classmates that if they ever needed a meal, they could come to my house. Obviously college students don't typically have a lot of money, so multiple times a week a bunch of us would gather at my house to eat. I'd use those nights to test out new recipes. This was another way I was inspired by my parents; they were so generous with everything we had. Even if finances were tight, we were able to give people food and bless them with produce. That's why I love cooking now. It's a way I can be generous with what I have."

JESUS PLACED AN EMPHASIS ON FELLOWSHIP, AND I THINK THAT SURPRISED PEOPLE AND MADE THEM FEEL SPECIAL.

Perhaps what has struck me most about Martha is the resilience of her intentionality. It is easy to pour your whole heart into a single meal—to build up anticipation for one particular event and give everything you have to make it special. But 365 days a year? That's a whole other level of extravagance. Over and over again, I have consistently witnessed Martha go the distance in extravagance. A batch of colorful, delicate macarons meticulously perfected is not a rare sight or taste around Martha. Neither is a lavish pound cake to celebrate the wedding of birthday of a dear friend. She is continuously communicating to people that they are worth what it takes to prepare something grand.

I have met Martha's smile in the kitchen, her hands busy at work but free of stress. I marvel at her balanced, peaceful demeanor. In an industry that is associated with cutthroat standards and a demanding, vigorous pace, Martha has maintained a patient and graceful perspective. She works with a diligence and kindness that is the real deal. This is love manifested in the kitchen. Martha has found Jesus in preparing a meal and setting the table. "When I set the table, I think of purposefully making a place for someone. Taking the time to love someone and to make a space for them is how Jesus loved His disciples. It is how He taught us to love. He was constantly feeding people, whether it was the 4,000 or the 5,000 or making breakfast for His disciples on the beach after their night of fishing. Jesus placed an emphasis on fellowship, and I think that surprised people and made them feel special. I think the most disarming thing you can do is to invite someone to share a meal with you. Getting to love someone by cooking a meal or making a space at the table gives them space to be known by people and the Lord."

Suddenly, I am in the Farmhouse kitchen again, drinking in the delicious smells and comforting sounds of family gathered together. Martha asks me how my day has been, while placing onions and mushrooms atop the rustic tart with ease. She invites me into conversation, revels in the small victories of my day and shares in my joy. Sliding the tart into the oven, she loosens her apron, looks me warmly in the eyes and says, "I'm so glad you've had a good day." Over the next several hours, a few of us gather around the table and indulge in the savory rustic tart. Laughter dances in the air with the aroma of the home-cooked meal. As I look at the faces around the table, my heart is moved. Martha catches my expression and gives me a knowing smile. These are the moments that have changed me—moments with Martha around the table.

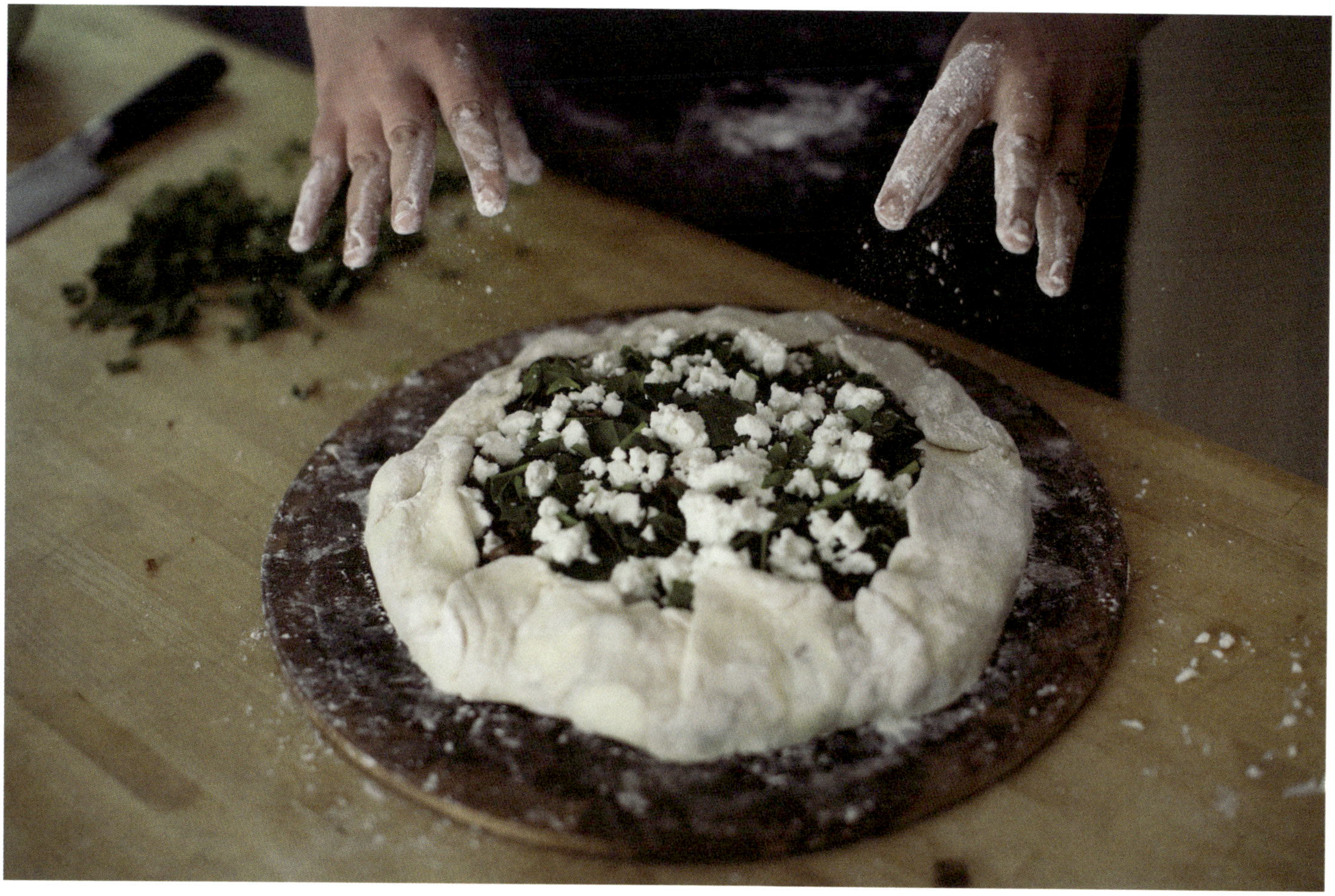

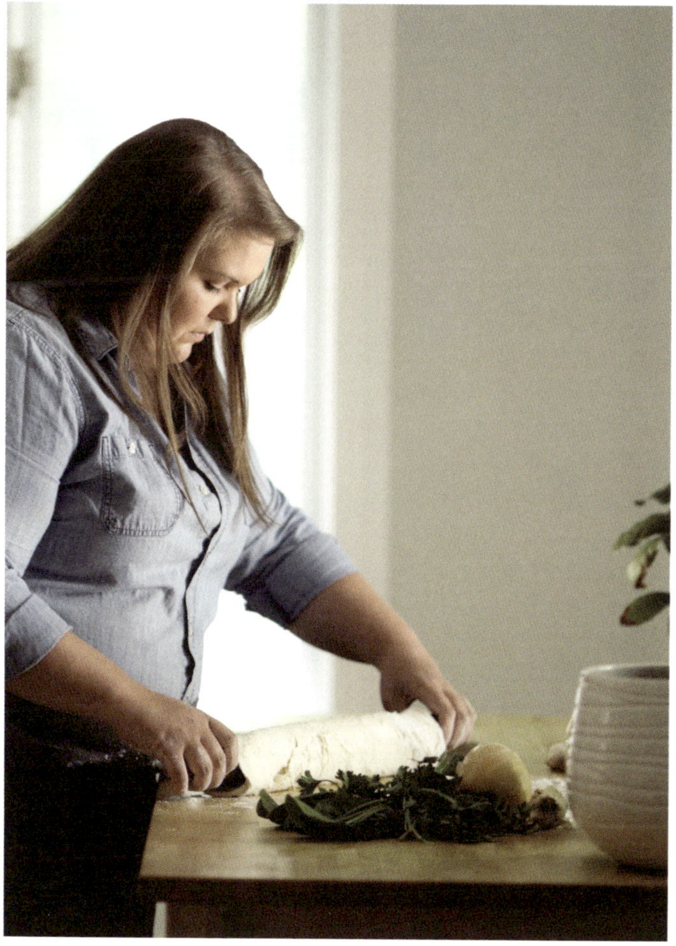

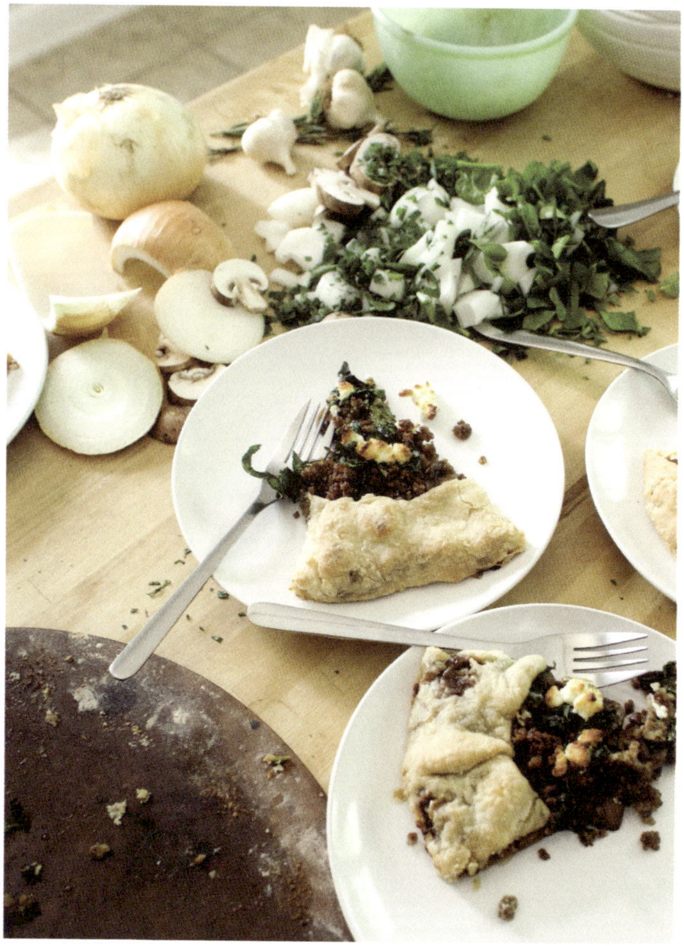

from the airplane window on a cloudless night

BY PHYLLIS UNKEFER

I blink my eyes.
Once. Then twice.
But still, I see them:

God and Abraham sitting.
Their legs, swung over the edge of the sky.
Side by side, where they've sat for centuries.
They lean forward, their eyes fixed.

See that? One whispers to the other
and points to some place in the world,
in Scotland or Morocco or maybe Brazil.
They hold their breath, lean farther in
and set their gazes on stars.

If you look from your airplane window on a cloudless night,
the earth will spread beneath you.
Stretched, black and shimmering, between horizons,
you'll find there's
a universe of stars.

Gold, white, amber, orange;
our cities are galaxies
of street lamps, houselights, fluorescent stadiums.
Our towns are constellations glimmering.
Lamplit windows.
Glinting building spires.
Golden highways of car headlights lace the night.
Our lives twinkle in clusters over the earth,
as if we were a firework held still against the dark.

God and Abraham peer down
and they look beyond.
Past the electric pulse, pumping through our power lines,
past the buzz and gleam of the civilized,
to the deeper lights.
The ones inside our chests.

In the mountains of Nepal,
where lamps don't burn for miles,
They still see us: the children of Light.

They know every soul is a burning bush.
Every mind, a lantern, where our thoughts fire and spark.
As we wash our dishes, tie our shoes, make our beds,
they see our quiet shining,
the glitter of our smiles.
The comets of our laughter streak the air.

And those flames that waver,
that dimly dance toward blowing out,
God's hands can reach and cup, if they ask Him.

We are the stars Abraham counts
joyously, one by one.
We are the white fire of his promise fulfilled.

We are the stars God wishes on,
and every evening, dreams to catch.
One by one, He finds us
till we spread across the earth. Luminous. Alive.
Daughters and sons of the Father of lights.
We are a whole universe of stars.

NO. 23

FREEDOM THROUGH TRUST

RECIPE FOR TRUST / BY JESSIE MILLER

I have an amazing little bird named Simeon. He is a parakeet with sherbet green and yellow feathers and bright blue cheeks. A friend of mine gave him to me about seven years ago as a surprise. I immediately felt how special he was and heard the Lord tell me, "This little bird will show you some keys about your heart and mine." Initially, Simeon was terrified of me. If I even put my hand near the cage, he would quickly move away. So I began to just sit by his cage, often times falling asleep, waiting for my bigness to not overwhelm his smallness. After a few weeks of this, he started coming to the side of the cage closest to me. He began to let me rub his little head through the cage. He began to believe I was safe. But I wanted more; I didn't just want to pet him through the cage. I wanted to hold him, to have him sit on my shoulder and watch him fly. The store he came from had clipped his wings, but I had been letting them grow out as I was taming him. My goal was to get him out of that cage. For weeks, I would put my hand in his cage a little bit everyday until he felt comfortable getting on it. The real catalyst to him choosing to crawl on my hand was actually a friendship ring! He was so fascinated by it that he would get on my hand and head straight for the ring. Simeon finally seemed comfortable. I thought, "Great, now he will just sit on my finger and come right out!" However, that was not the case. Getting him through that little cage door was just not happening. So with a careful heart of desire to see him free, I wrapped my hand around his squiggling body and pulled him out. As I uncurled my fingers, he began to fly! He flew and flew until he landed back on my hand, which was now the most comforting thing he recognized in the wide-open space. I could feel his little heart beating fast with excitement and his little lungs drinking in gulps of free air.

Our Father is so much larger and more complex than we can comprehend. Yet He sits at the door of our heart so full of love and desire to bond with us. He longs for companionship with us and has unfazed patience to build the trust it requires. He waits for us to approach Him, His distance never far away, but close. He comes in familiar ways so we can recognize Him. As we say yes, He moves even closer, and His hand becomes more evident in our lives. We can choose to fear it, or we can choose to bravely climb on and see what happens. In His kindness, He offers friendships—people to encourage us that trusting Him is worth the risk. Just as my goal was to see Simeon free, so the Father feels about us. He longs for the deeper bond, the one outside of the safety of what we know, where there is freedom to meet and freedom to touch. He wraps His hand around our squiggling circumstances and puts us out into the open air. You can trust Him as you open your heart. He is the kindest liberator. His hand is always present to guide you home, and His protective eyes of love are attentive, watching for anything that might disrupt your flight. He is bringing you to freedom by winning your heart.

Prompt: Father, what are the ways you are taming my heart? Show me what it looks like to take the next step in trusting you. Journal His Response.

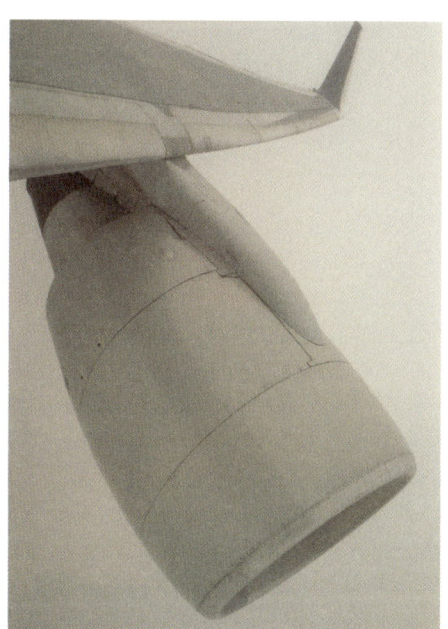

PERSPECTIVE
BY MELISSA HELSER

I fly a lot. From 30,000 feet in the air, I must choose to see in a whole new way. Everytime I get a window seat I practice letting joy sweep over me. The far-off beauty challenges, changes and inspires my perspective. It is high up here. The sky is endless. This collection represents a few of the 500 pictures I have taken from the sky of clouds, oceans, fields, snowy landscapes, sunsets and rivers on my phone.

PHOTOS TAKEN ON THE I-PHONE 6
FROM AN AIRPLANE WINDOW

SUSPENDED IN SAFETY

RECIPE FOR TRUST IN THE SILENCE / BY LINDSAY VANCE

It was the first true Saturday in spring, the kind that makes you feel like you were created for adventures outside and soaking up the sun. We made the trek to Pilot Mountain in the North Carolina foothills to spend the day gaining a higher perspective. We were going rock climbing.

Watching my experienced climber friends go before me churned an excitement in my belly. Their quick and decided movements from one crack in the rock to the next made climbing look effortless. I shimmied into my harness and snapped tight my helmet so I could begin. I was no more than five feet off the ground before my excitement turned into fear. I realized that watching my friends execute a route just minutes before did not mean I had any idea what I was doing. My fiancé, Zac, began to coach me through each move from the ground, staying a few steps ahead of me so that he could discern the best route for me. Palms sweaty and arms outstretched, I grappled my way slowly to the top. By the time I reached the ground again, I collapsed in the dirt, laughing relief and disbelief into the air. It was a lot harder than I'd imagined!

As the day went on, I made three more successful climbs to the top of the rock face. With each climb, I was empowered to make choices based on my own experience and take greater risks. My heart soared with courage like the birds of prey that lived in the nearby sanctuary. From the top, the view was endless. There were equal parts sky and land. The juxtaposition of the distant beauty and the near reality that I was suspended in the air made me come alive.

My final ascension was up a route called a chimney, a giant crevice between two rocks. I moved like brush strokes with precision, firm hands and swift legs. About three-quarters of the way up, however, I became stumped with where I should go next. Rocks cornered me in on three sides and blocked my vision upward. I shouted down the mountain for help, "What should I do?" Silence echoed, and suddenly I felt unsafe.

Why wasn't Zac answering? Each second that passed chipped away at my confidence. Why did I think this was a good idea? Hanging on for my life, I peered back, trying to make eye contact. I am definitely going to fall. Stillness and silence.

As I was contemplating the fear of a tremendous fall, I heard the voice of the Holy Spirit speak to my own spirit, "Where are you sitting, Lindsay?" I looked at my harness girding my legs and then traced the rope attached to it up the rock face and back down to Zac again. I could feel the Holy Spirit's grin widening. Grace! In the realest sense, I was "hemmed in behind and before," completely dependent on the one holding the rope. I was seated in grace! The silence of the moment did not define the safety of my life. Floods of truth washed over my mind. I couldn't fall even if I were to let go.

As the Holy Spirit testified to my spirit, confidence began welling up in my heart again. Where initially I interpreted Zac's silence as reason to panic, I now understood what he was communicating without words. *He is silent because he believes in me,* I thought. *I can make a brave move.*

Maybe you are in a season where the Lord is responding with silent instruction. Maybe He is not shouting out your next move. The Lord's silence does not mean He is absent. He knows you are seated in grace. Sometimes the way God teaches us is to let us make a brave choice—not because He doesn't want to help, but because He knows that practicing His truths will make them real in our hearts. Zac could have guided me through the chimney with perfect instruction and I would have ended the day successfully. But because he chose to guide me with silence, I gained something far more valuable. He trusts me. I trust myself.

Prompt: God is raising up confident sons and daughters in Christ who believe in the power of their choice. Sit with God and ask Him to bring to mind a truth He has been revealing to your heart. A truth can be as simple as "God is a good Father" or "God does not leave me." Where is God inviting you to work out this truth in your life by making a brave and powerful choice? Maybe the choice is simply believing in yourself. Maybe it's a choice that calls you to action. Let God speak to you and journal His voice.

SONG *of* REDEMPTION

BY MOLLY KATE SKAGGS

Broken.
She carried the burden of tired wings,
of flustered feathers that seemed to weep for
themselves.

Exhausted.
She was the home of a heart nearly collapsing,
and Strife was a frequent guest who overstayed
his welcome.

Measured.
She gazed upon the other birds who were free
and soared effortlessly —
boundless was the sky in their hearts.

Ashamed.
And she — what was she exactly?
A pitiful excuse
for one made to fly.

Offended.
She hurled her angry questions to their faces —
"what makes you so special anyway?"

Understood.
With knowing smiles, their encouragement led
her to reach out to the Wind —
"Go ask Wind. He will tell you everything."

Afraid.
She faced the unknown unpredictability of who
she could not see —
"Can you hear me? Do you even hear me?"

Surrounded.
He suddenly came to her in a mighty swirl,
rushes of great, violent joy burst all around her.

Received.
He spoke of a much longed-for day and how it
had arrived —
"You have called for me, and I have come."

Known.
His cool breeze wiped her bitter tears,
compassion holding close her tiny frame like
strong unseen arms.

Befriended.
She learned that the soaring life required what is
most precious —
trust is the opening of wings to the Wind.

Beloved.
The only way a bird with broken wings learns
how to fly again.
A beautiful dependency on Love.

Permission

BY CHRIS MILLER / PAINTING BY JUSTINA STEVENS

I am a corporal with wings,
not like the lifeless lines
etched on fabric frames
with wings outstretched and
working together.
I was a song in the air
that longed for home,
called by a deeper sound,
my flight plan altered forever.

She is my coda,
the beauty of always belonging
and humbly returning.

She is like the mountainside
that keeps beckoning me
back to the water's edge
to drink deep
and remember my name.
Like the gravity in each waking breath
she woke me with a symphony of
yes, yes, YES.

At the altar we stood with wings suspended,
giving permission to the newfound spring
forever falling from our hymnal
into a living, breathing harmony.

Surely, this is what it looks like to fly
in one formation,
as four wings find the same pace
our rhythms fold into one.

We are the lovebirds
who found home in this sky.

NO. 25

SOARING IN THE WORKPLACE

RECIPE FOR RENEWING YOUR MINDSET / BY JESSIE MILLER

"If any of you lacks wisdom, you should ask God, who gives generously to all without finding fault, and it will be given to you" (James 1:5, NIV).

"Love the Lord God with all our passion and prayer and intelligence and energy" (Mark 12:30, MSG).

Do you ever feel like your job holds you back from soaring with the Father? As a high school biology teacher at a high-needs school, I certainly have. I often asked, "How can I soar in a place where I feel so little control over the circumstances surrounding me?" I felt like I couldn't get any higher or freer in my job because I couldn't get all the people around me to buy into the plans I knew were possible for them. I felt stuck on the ground, unable to be successful in the Lord's sight, because my students were not performing as I so boldly hoped they would. I desperately wanted to give the Lord the gift of a fully transformed classroom. I found myself devastated with my own shortcomings and crushed that God wouldn't step in as I thought He should. In my eyes, the Lord was looking for evidence that my redeemed spirit was accomplishing all it was made for, and I was failing this expectation. I became so tired of being out-of-control and yet highly responsible for how things were going. I blamed my job for keeping me from flying and the Lord for not helping me accomplish what I was so sure He wanted.

This is what happens when we do not ask the Father for His vision. I was not fully united with His viewpoint for me at work. Instead, I assumed. I decided, back in a deep corner of my heart, that in order to really please Him, I had to surprise Him with my victory. I presumed I already knew what He wanted. If He would just do His part, I could take care of the rest. Crushed by my own fear of failing, I begged Him to manipulate the students I served to obey me, and my colleagues to understand me. I judged myself by my own false expectations.

In His kindness, God would not affirm my false assumptions. My freedom to soar would not come through control or ease. It would come through trust, vision and connection. Our jobs are meant to be a wide-open opportunity for communion, not a performance ritual. The Father longs for connection instead of results. In all my strivings to feel victorious, I was missing the value of simple opportunities to love and serve Him by loving and serving His children. I expected Him to change others, but instead He wanted to change my view of them. He invited me to start seeing Him in plain interactions with other people. He challenged me to let Him work with me, instead of trying to show Him all I was able to accomplish. As I opened up and let go of my own expectations, I started feeling His unwavering pleasure again. He was able to clarify His true desires for me in the workplace, and this clarity has set me free to soar without needing control.

Prompt: Pray, "Father, what are some expectations that I am working under that you have not placed on me? Please show me what truly brings you joy when I am in the workplace." Journal His response.

NO. 26

MOTIVATED TO LOVE HIM

RECIPE FOR JOY OF SALVATION / BY KAYE SHAVER

I love a good motivational speech—not the cheesy, predictable kind, but the kind that makes you want to stand on your feet and shout, "Yes!" I would love to write such a speech for you here, but I am not a motivational speaker. I can only tell you my story of "first love" with Jesus, in hopes that you feel truly motivated to love Him today.

Long ago, as a high school graduate, I was trapped in a pit of darkness. Fear and anxiety of the future were my constant companions. I didn't know how to break free. The hippie culture in the 1970s, which seemed so genuine in the beginning, soon turned ugly and wrapped its monstrous tentacles around me. One day my friends and I found ourselves in a house by the woods, and a strange thing happened. A Christian was there. He asked if he could pray for us. Sure, we didn't care whether he prayed or whether he didn't. We stood in a circle while he prayed. We just listened, and then we left. I was driving home by myself listening to music when all of a sudden Heaven invaded my VW! I had the marvelous, life-changing revelation that Jesus was real.

"He is real. He is real. He is real!" I was stunned. His love began to capture my heart. "I am loved. I am loved. I am loved by this real Jesus." I was completely immersed in His love. Scales dropped from my eyes, and I could see. The whole world looked cleaner and so beautiful. I was taken from death and placed in Life. I was so clueless about the ways of the Lord that I didn't understand what had happened. During the next two weeks, I made my way to a church in a barn and met a minister named Tom Watson. I began to hear words of life and truth, and I gave my life to Jesus.

My salvation has been the greatest miracle of my life. Satan lost his grip on me! God took a wretched creature and transformed me. He gave me life so abundant. He has carried me in the hard places and danced with me in the celebrations of life. Jesus has been my Knight in shining armor, my Prince on the white horse, the One who woke me with a kiss, rescuing me from death. I will forever praise Him for His tender mercies and grace.

Prompt: Think about the first moments you fell in love with Jesus and were saved by His grace. Pray, "Lord, thank you for my moment of 'first love' with you! Thank you for saving my soul. Help me to live from the overflow of the joy of my salvation. Help me to work out my salvation daily by receiving your love. Amen."

embrace the return

"SINCE THIS IS THE KIND OF LIFE WE HAVE CHOSEN, THE LIFE OF THE SPIRIT, LET US MAKE SURE THAT WE DO NOT JUST HOLD IT AS AN IDEA IN OUR HEADS OR A SENTIMENT IN OUR HEARTS, BUT WORK OUT ITS IMPLICATIONS IN EVERY DETAIL OF OUR LIVES."

GALATIANS 5:25, MSG

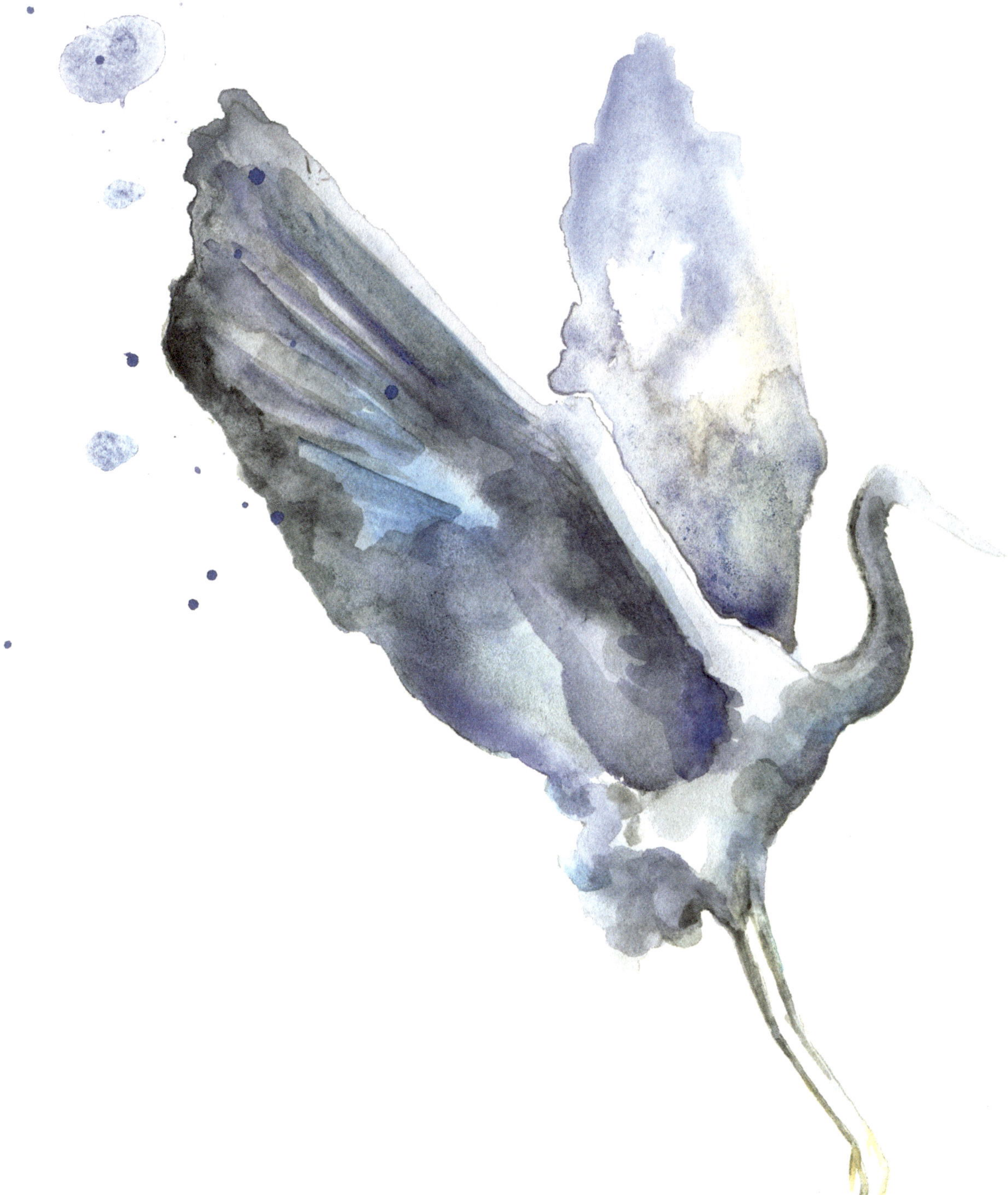

NO. 27

LANDING

RECIPE FOR SUSTAINABILITY / BY LUKE SKAGGS

Life is both moments of ascending and descending. Sometimes the wind will blow, and we will ascend to the heights. Sometimes the air will become still, causing our descent. I've learned that being carried up high by the wind is just as important as coming back down to a home God and I have built together on solid ground. This has been a great challenge. When you have not built home with the Father, there is no delight in landing because you are essentially coming back to nothing. My journey has been one of the Father teaching me to surrender to the wind and its change.

I would regularly go on tours around the world playing music with dear friends I love so deeply. We would watch our music and friendship reveal the nature of Jesus to people's lives. Talk about ascent! But then the moment would come when we'd say goodbye and return to our homes till the next time. Descent. This descent for me consistently looked like a crash landing. After many seasons of crashing I knew that something wasn't right. I needed the Father to show me a better way.

I made a very bold and scary choice, and for two months my twenty-four-year-old self decided to hit the pause button on all my touring plans. I allowed my heart to slow down and return to Jesus by attending the 18 Inch Journey in 2013. That's when the Father and I began to build home together in my heart. In those two months, I realized my home was on the road doing big, great things in the name of Jesus. Those were the places I saw His smile and felt His delight. But when it was over, what I came back to was not a home in God. I came back to the mundane. Here, I could not see His smile or feel His delight over me. He began to reveal His love and affection toward me even when I was grounded and doing nothing with my gifts. This home He built for me was solely made up of His love and had nothing to do with what I could do or produce for Him. These were the bricks that built my true home in God. Now when I begin to descend from the sky into the quiet stillness of Earth, I know how to land in His heart.

Landing is nothing more than giving in to a change in the wind, letting myself come back down into the well-established home I have built with the Father. Landing will always feel like a crash if we have not allowed Jesus to make His home in our hearts. If we don't invite Him to become our consistent sustainability in the loud and quiet moments, we will be homeless.

Prompt: Find a piece of paper and fold a paper airplane. Go to an open space and fly your plane. Watch how it ascends and descends. While you do this, ask the Father to speak to you about soaring and landing. Let Him to show you places where you haven't learned to land properly. Repent for only looking to the ascent to sustain your life outside of Him. Invite Him to show you a better way. Unfold your paper airplane and journal His voice.

GRANDFATHER'S HANDS

POEM AND PHOTO BY SYDNEE MELA

Words become quiet.
Thoughts become still.
The room stands at attention.
As my heart moves with zeal.
Forward I move. How this lights up your face.
Your hand reaches out.
Catching us in grace.

Years upon years for this moment to be.
History woven in an instant.
Love filling my tank.
Security in your fingertips.
Heartache in your pain.
Touch that speaks louder than words,
louder than anything could say.

These hands taught me to grow.
Taught me not to be afraid.
Enduring years to meet me here.
Wrinkles rewarding the journey.
Showing their age, never ashamed.
Life is for those who live it and don't
throw it away.

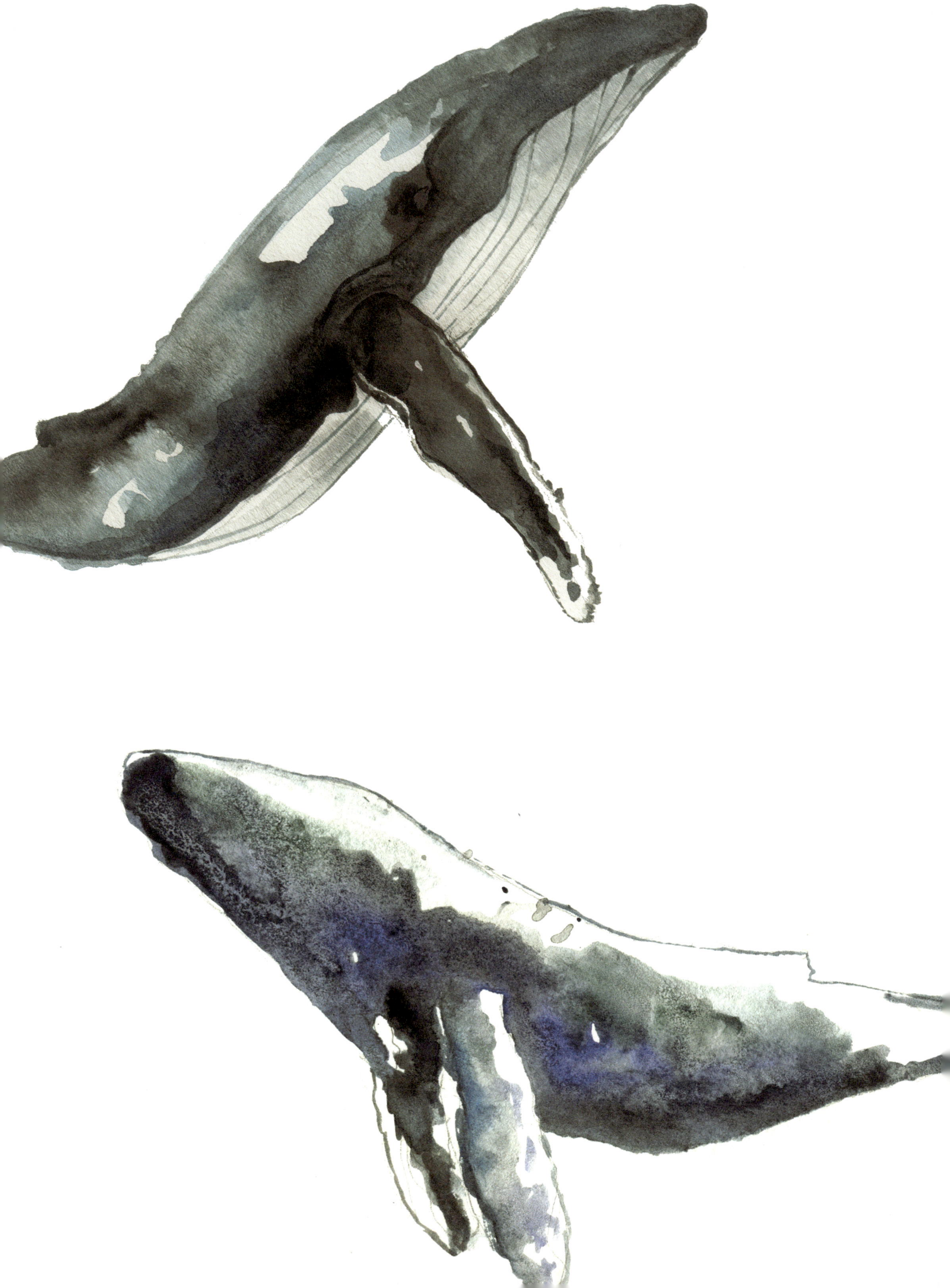

a MIGRATION of WHALES

BY MELISSA HELSER
PAINTINGS BY LINDSAY VANCE

What is the grandeur of the giants of the sea? When they arise out of the depths, I only see a small piece of their beauty. Still they strike awe. Sitting on black shores of hardened fire, I watch for any sign of them— for a shooting through water, a billowing of their huge dark frames, a massive tail rising and falling. I never see all of them. Seeing part of them lets me know they are there, under the surface, beyond my world. They exist whether I see them or not. I align myself with faith rooted in knowing; knowing they are real. Every moment I breathe, they breathe.

What is faith? Faith is trust in what I know is real, even if I can't see it manifest when I want it to. I look, patiently waiting, suspended in time. Sometimes it emerges from the depths when I am not even looking. These faith-filled moments catch my attention while I am immersed in another thought. Faith rises up from the depths and reminds me that He is always present. Maturity is believing and not doubting. It is believing that the Giver of Life is always here, always moving, always engaging. He is always shocking me, always surprising me. What if I grow to a place where I am astonished, but not surprised?

THE WHALES MIGRATE EVERY YEAR. THEY ALWAYS COME TO THE LONE ISLANDS IN THE MIDDLE OF THE PACIFIC OCEAN. I AM ASTONISHED, BUT NOT SURPRISED.

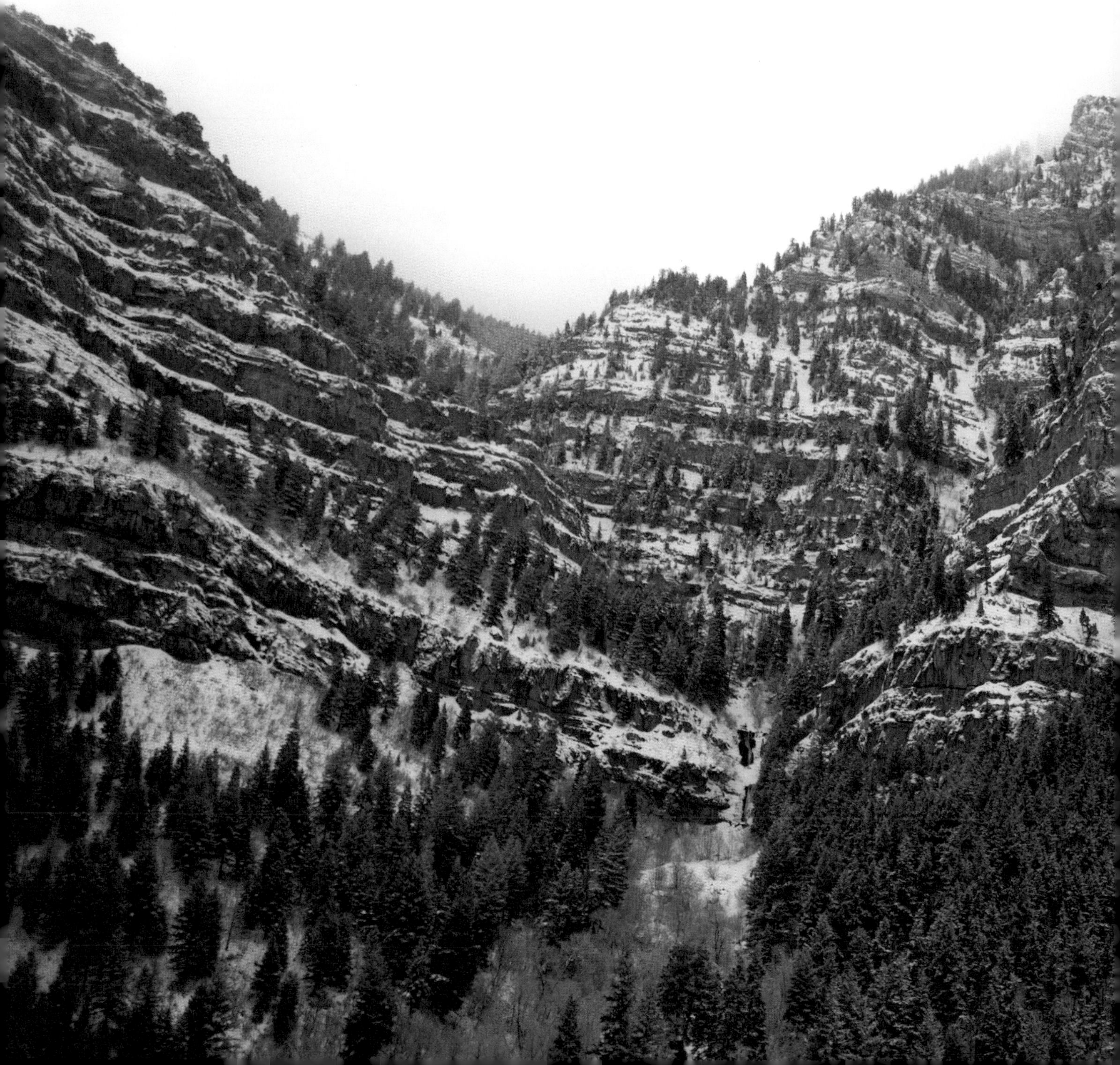

"THE MORE HEAVEN COMES TO EARTH, THE MORE THE EARTH WILL LOOK LIKE FAMILY."

—JONATHAN DAVID HELSER

NO. 28

WONDER

RECIPE FOR DELIGHT / BY PHYLLIS UNKEFER / PAINTING BY JUSTINA STEVENS

For weeks, I heard a single word drop repeatedly into my mind before I finally asked, "Lord, what do you mean?" The word was wonder, and I heard it in very non-wondrous moments: while washing dishes, folding laundry, typing an email for work. I love the word. Its six letters feel tremendously full; brimming with life, shot through with vastness and mystery.

The Father answered me that morning, "Phyllis, the disposition of wonder will remind your heart that there's meaning to life right now." "Right now" was a challenging season for me. A time of running headlong into fears and facing shame, with all its counterfeit shadows. Jesus assured me of His ability to lead me through it; I'm watching Him do it even now. And wonder was part of His joyful strategy.

The wondrous can be found anywhere. As for me, I'm most often drawn outside. I take a walk to find the thing that moves me. To feel the wind. Watch the tall grass sway. Gasp as the turtle's striped head lifts above water and quickly tucks back under, his curiosity satisfied. See the airplanes carve white streams of possibility into the sky that implore me to keep my hope as they slowly fade. And then there's my favorite place: the bench swing under the trees. Here, I lie on my back and look up into sunlit leaves. The way the light spills and leaves glow in cascades, golden-rimmed, vibrant green—I can't help but marvel. This canopy is an uproar of radiance! A fire on every branch. I stare until I'm convinced that part of heaven must be on the end of a stem.

The first day I set out to engage wonder, I sat on this same swing. I was tracing the leaves and listening to the wind when—who knew that a woodpecker would fly in? He landed on the tree directly in front of me with his head blazing red and his body speckled black and white. Sometimes adoration is instant. I watched him casually stroll all the way up the trunk. I held my breath and sat silent with delight. By the time he flew away, thanksgiving had swept through me. I'd been overtaken by the Father's smile.

Wonder fills up the soul! It causes our hearts to swell into sails that can catch God's Wind. Wonder is the choice to perceive His beauty and love in the world, His intention and design. It's to enjoy Him. We cannot exhaust it. Jesus told me, while I studied a cicada's mother-of-pearl wings, "In thirty years, this still won't get old." Wonder reminds me that nothing is random or wasted. Meaning is woven everywhere. I can more graciously walk through the mundane and difficult parts of life by practicing the disposition of wonder. So on many afternoons, I spend an hour on that old swing feeling God's goodness rise inside me. I walk back home, restored.

Prompt: Set your questions and worries in the Father's hands, and take time to engage wonder. Go outside. Find the things that move you. Notice your simple delight. Feel the Father's smile. Write down what you saw. Ask Him, "How are you present in my wonder?"

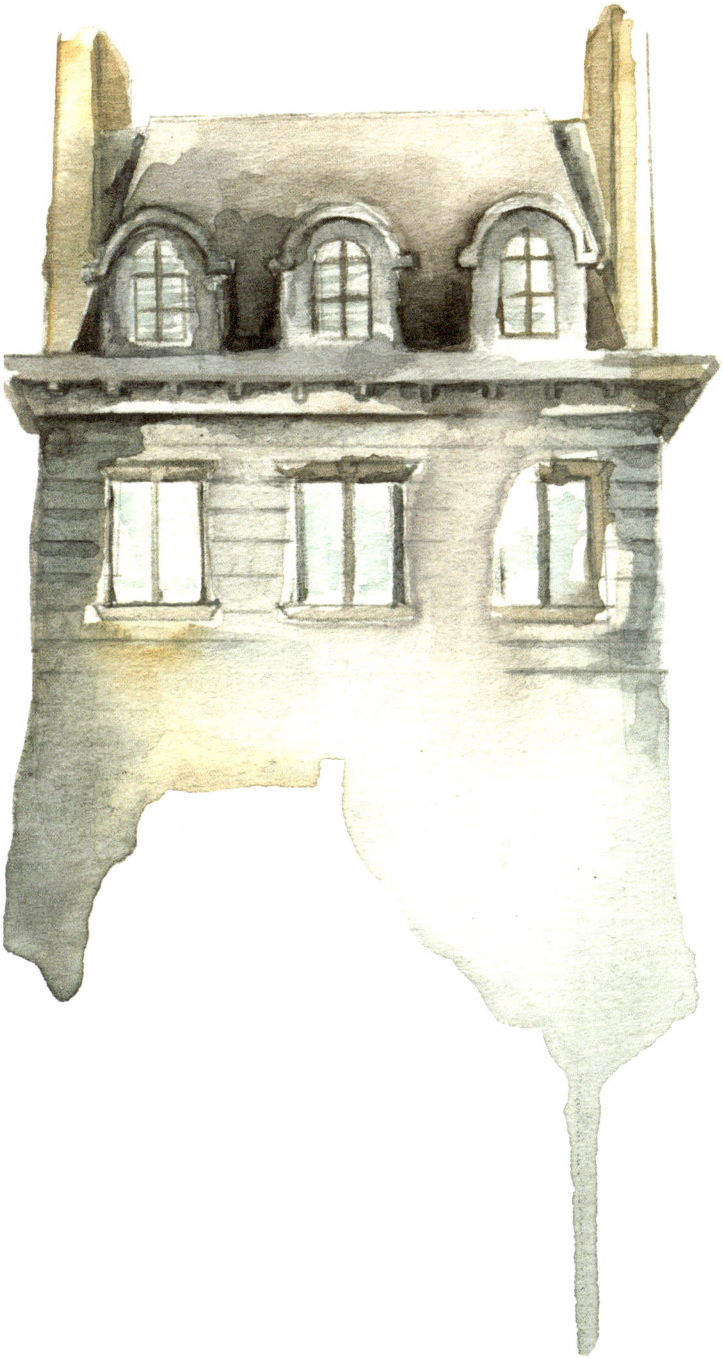

SLOWING DOWN

REFLECTIONS FROM THE WHITE CLIFFS *of* ENGLAND
WRITING AND PHOTOGRAPHY BY MELISSA HELSER

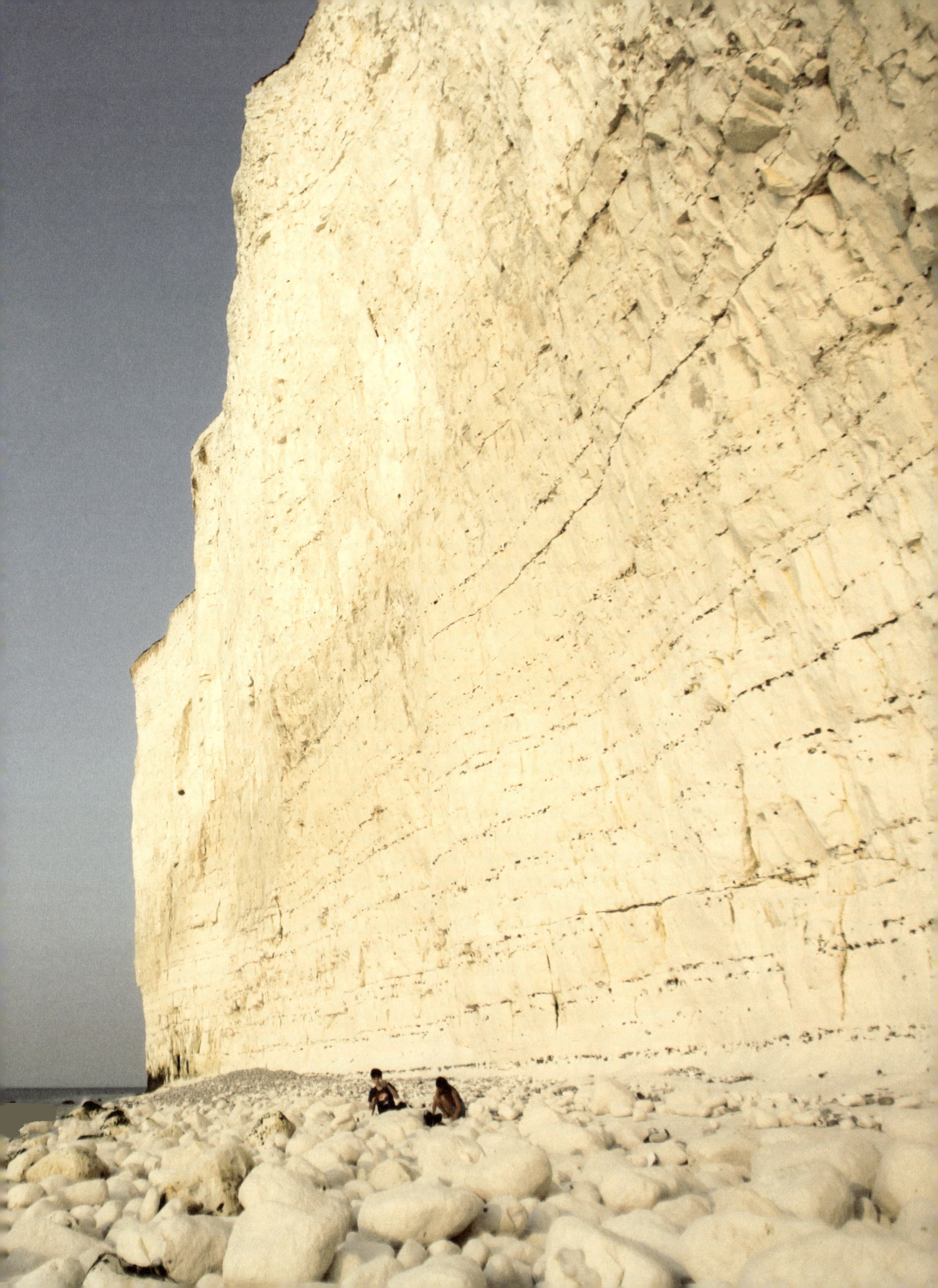

Slowing down has completely changed the way I do life. The greatest place I have learned to stop and recognize beautiful moments is in my role as a mother. Our pace of life can dictate so much. We sometimes stop being present in moments that really matter and rush through moments that are intended to build foundations for our children that only we can build.

I remember the moment we stepped onto the white rock beach in the South of England. We looked left and right and were astounded by the towering white cliffs of beauty. The air was crisp and clear. The waves slowly approached the shore. As they hugged the white stones, water became cloudy and took back a part of the shore with it. An invitation came to me as I walked down that beach: "Will you slow down…will you build home in this moment?" Slowing down takes a very intentional effort. It requires an honesty of acknowledging that you are in a hurry. Most of the time I think we don't even know what we are hurrying for. I am growing in my love for the invitation. The Holy Spirit is always sending us invitations. He is always desiring to teach us how to live and breathe and engage this glorious life. He isn't pushy. He is incredibly patient. The more I mature in my understanding of who the Father is and what He is like, the more I love the moments when He comes and invites me deeper. The fruit of my slowing down is an awareness of the presence of a loving God in every second of my life, no matter how grand or how simple.

Each of us went into our own way of processing the beauty of the beach around us. Jonathan sat and stared. Cadence began to build and chisel and see if he could break the rocks open. Haven got dirty discovering that the stones were balls of chalk and would rub off on everything. I took pictures, lots of pictures. We were all astonished, and as I looked around, I knew we were in a slow-motion moment. Each of us was pulling life out of the silence. It goes down in our family history as one of the most breathtaking experiences we have ever had. Every time I make a choice to listen to the still small voice, I lay another stone on the foundation of our family. Every time I don't rush moments that are meant to linger, I imprint on my kids' hearts, "Life is worth loving. Life is worth enjoying."

One of my clearest memories of slowing down and listening to the Lord was when my son turned thirteen. He cried and said to us, "I don't want to grow up. I don't want life to change." I immediately tried to think of something great to say to soothe his emotions. I wonder why we rush through tears. Grieving is one of the greatest gifts that the Father gives us to properly transition seasons of life. If we speed through these moments we miss the opportunity of a face-to-face encounter with the Comforter. He is the God of comfort, the God who meets us in the middle of our tears. Thankfully, I felt the still small voice and refrained from explaining away my son's heartache. I heard the Lord say, "Let him grieve his childhood; he loved it so much he doesn't want to leave this place of beauty." I took a deep breath and wept with him; I didn't want it to change either. I never thought I would love it so much.

Without the rhythms of slowing down and building strong foundations, I would have rushed through some of the greatest moments my life will ever know. I want to look back on my life and remember the beauty, the light, the sounds, the taste. I want to remember the tears and laughter. I want to remember the silence.

I challenge you to stop, take a deep breath and pray this: Holy Spirit, slow down the rhythm of the way I think and engage life. I invite you to make me aware of moments that I'd usually hurry through. Jesus, give me eyes to see what I before could not see. Make me aware when I am rushing, and teach me to practice the fruit of the Spirit that is self-control. Empower me with the courage to pause and make powerful choices for my life, believing wholeheartedly that you never grow weary of helping me. I declare that YOU ARE A GOOD FATHER. Help me live a full life with a keen understanding of your presence always. You are the Giver of all good things. I receive in this moment the pace of Heaven.

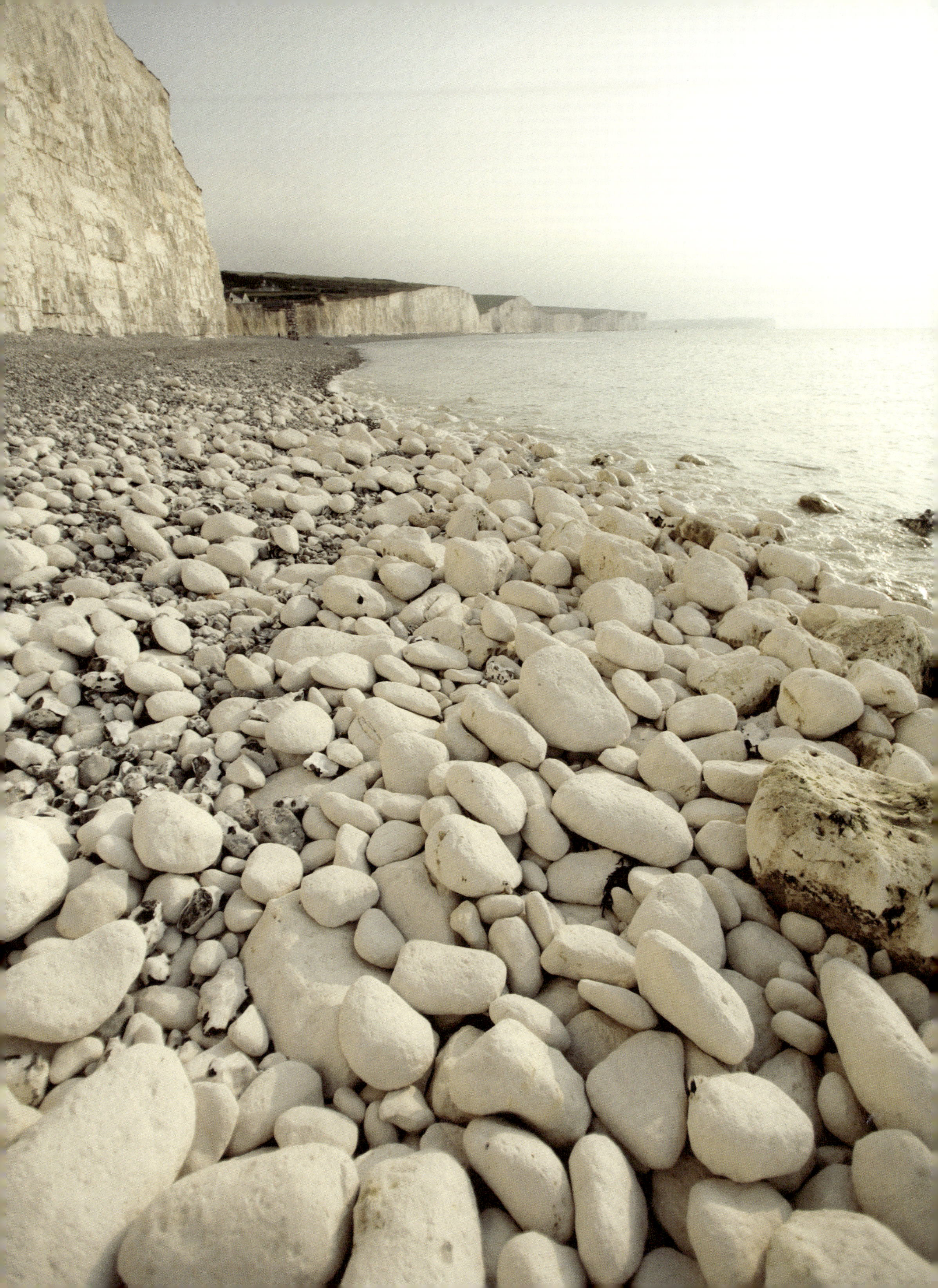

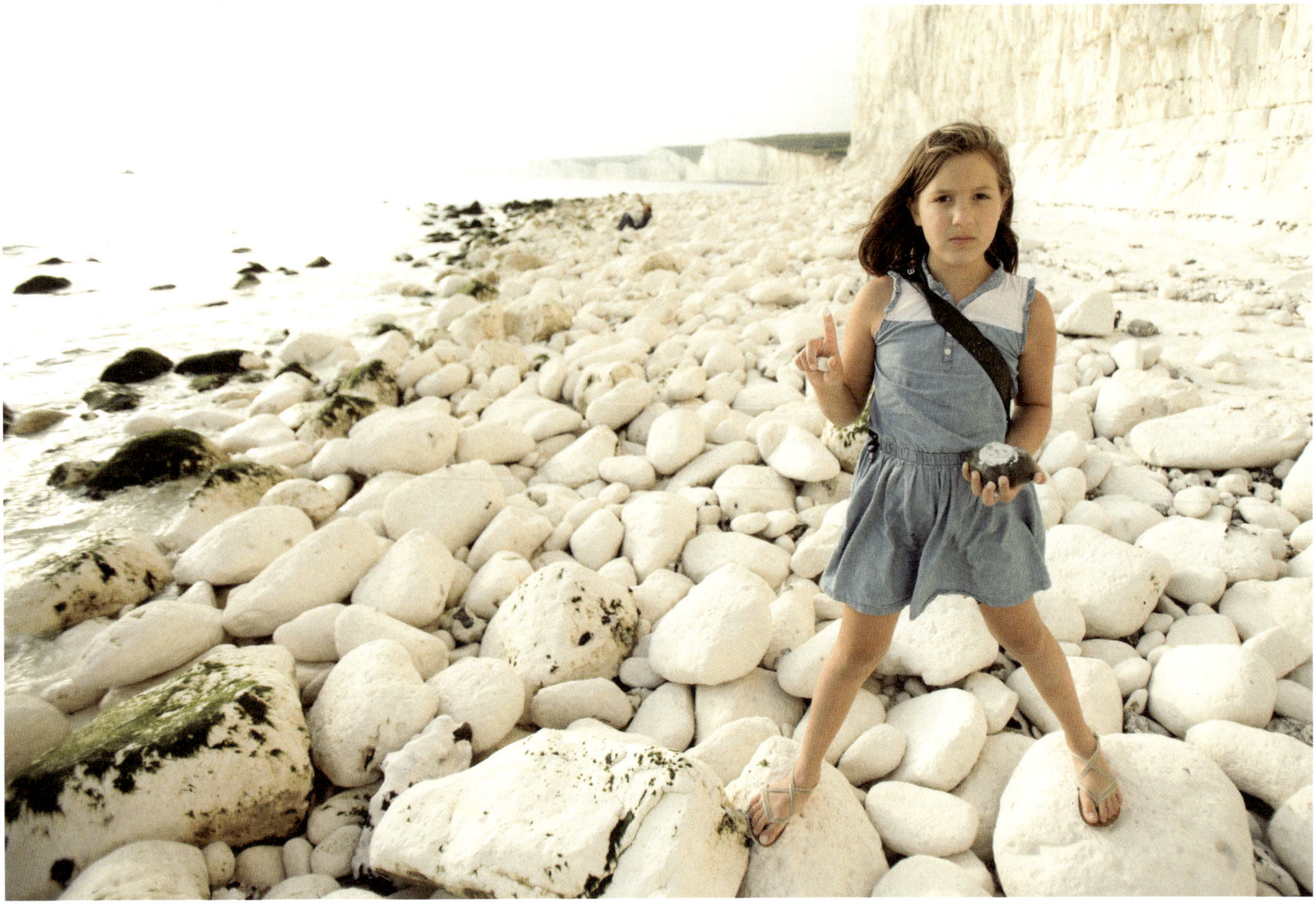
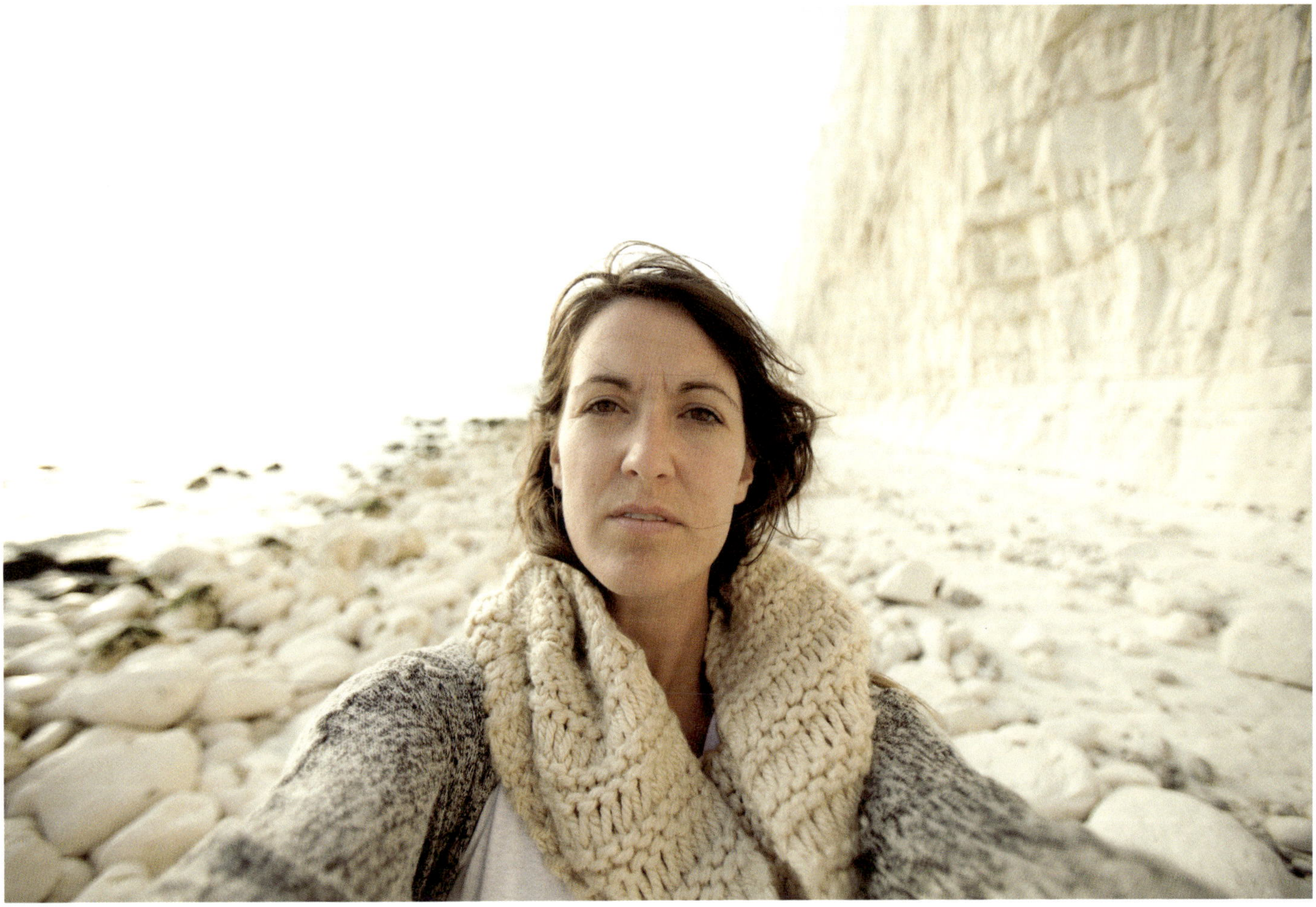

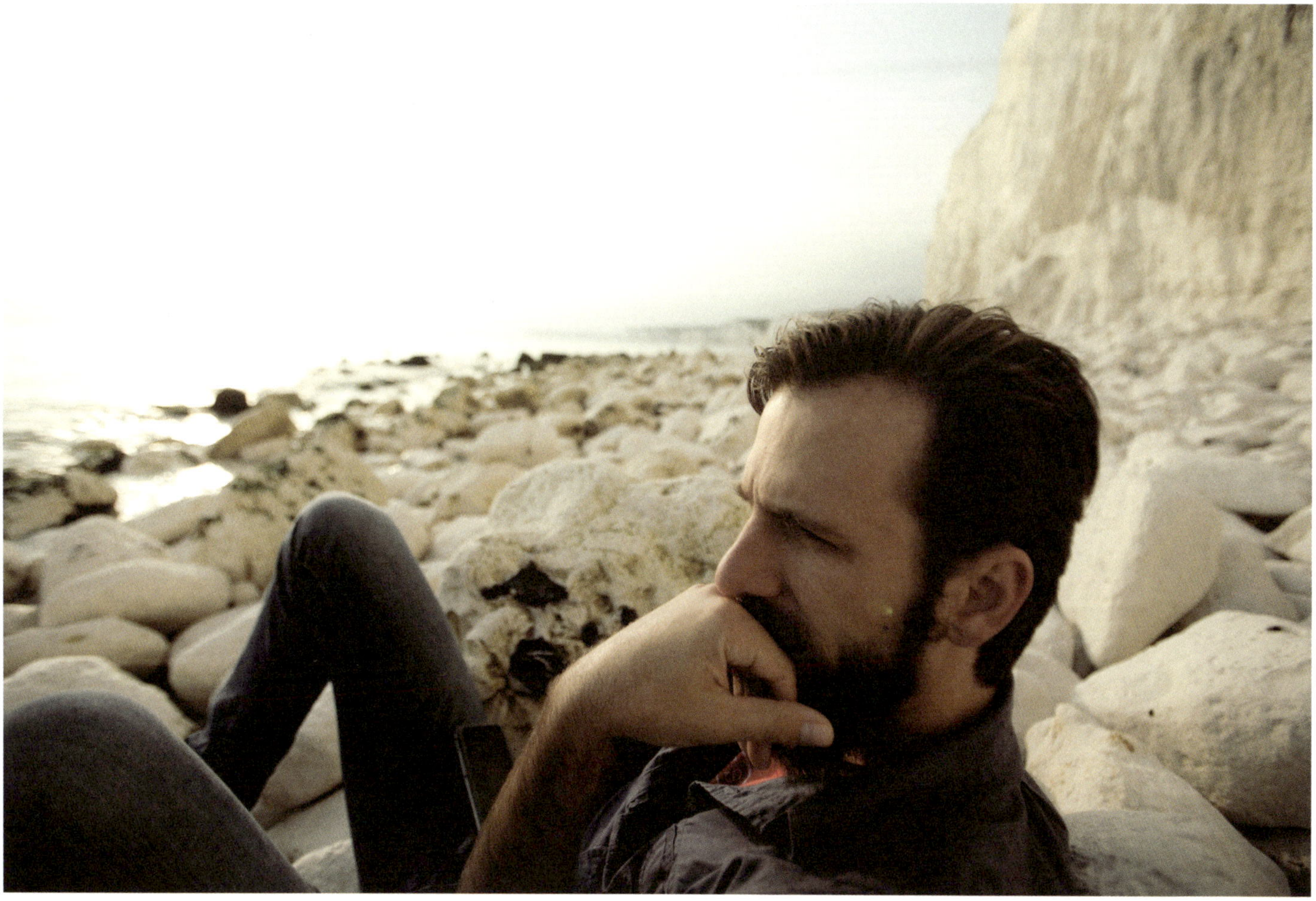

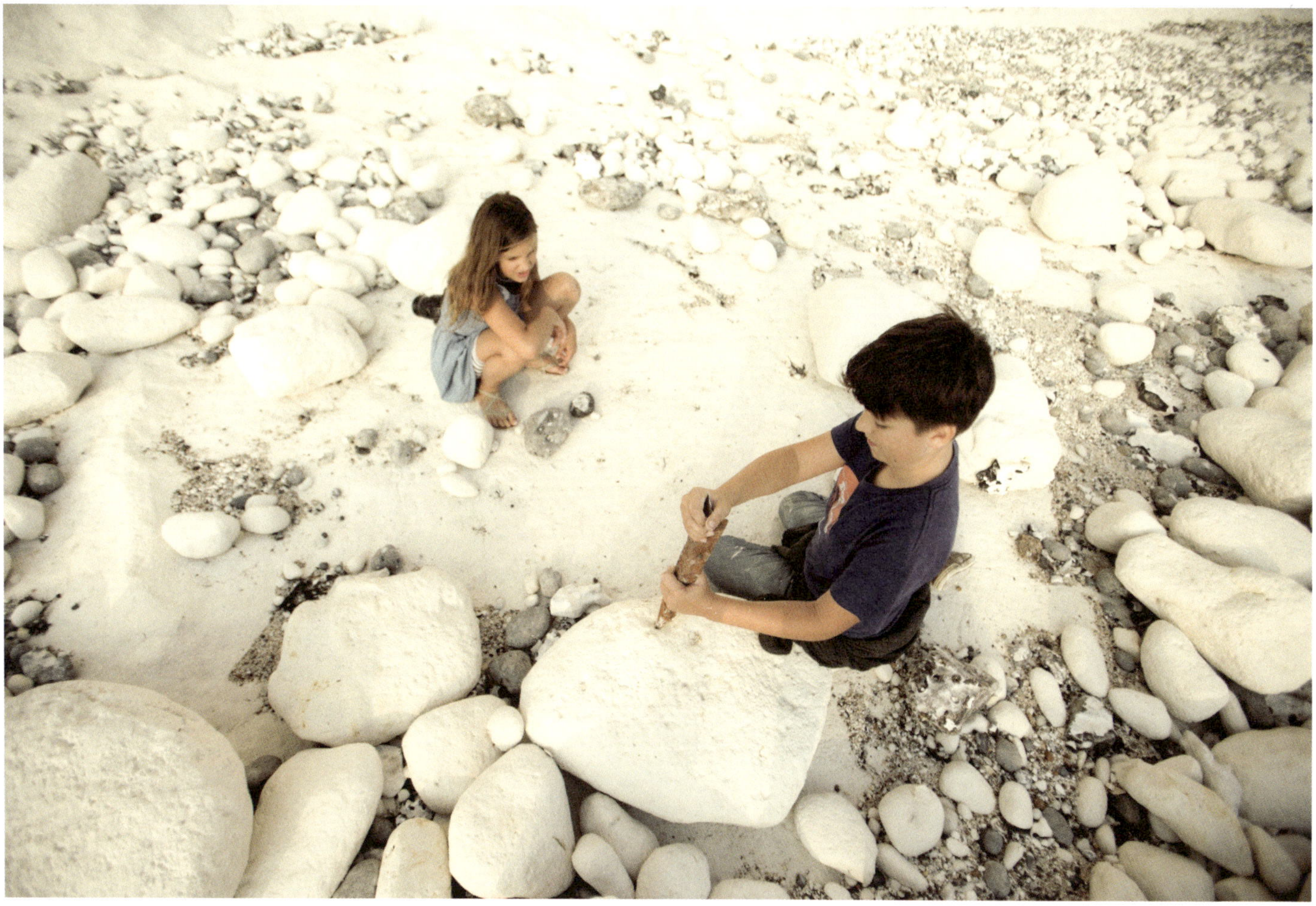

NO. 29

CANCEL THE DISTANCE

PROMPT BY MORGAN CAMPBELL

Our lives are not linear. They are ever-changing, moving and evolving as we listen and respond to the voice of the Creator. The people our paths cross with during one season might be completely different from another, but the Lord binds and sustains fruitful relationships through His faithfulness. He is constantly working on our behalf to build bridges and interweave our stories.

In one season of my life, I moved to three different states within a span of nine months. My life was constantly in transition, and I felt confused and afraid for what would happen in my significant friendships. I was fearful that I would lose intimacy and connection and that a new community wouldn't arise. In that season, the Father spoke to me and said, "Morgan, I am fighting for your friendships more than you are." Although this season was difficult, I can clearly see that there was more growth and intentionality in my heart that wouldn't have developed if I hadn't learned to trust the Lord to cancel the distance and keep me connected. The Lord was fighting for my heart to feel surrounded by love—to feel sustained in family.

Ask the Father to remind you of all the people in your life who are standing with you, near and far. Picture their faces and remember the ways in which they have transformed and shaped your journey. Write down the people and places that come to mind and plot the web of names on a map to encourage your heart and remember the Father's ability to cancel the distance.

NO. 30

CHILDLIKENESS

PROMPT BY MEGHAN HOCKADAY

Throughout my four years of college, I nannied a little girl named Lucy. Lucy and I spent our afternoons inside imagined palaces, building protective barriers to defend ourselves against monsters and dragons, sometimes even facing them head-on in battle. Our only weapons were wooden swords and plastic wands, and we met our feigned foes head-on with shouts of exuberant joy. It was a delight to spend so much time with this ray of sunshine. When so much of my life in that season was dedicated to studying, writing papers and giving presentations, I was given the privilege of exercising joy and wonder in a universe created by a little girl. A girl who, at such a young age, somehow knew so much more about the world than I did. Lucy was a gift at a time in my life when I simply needed to remember what it was like to engage in child-like joy.

Think back on the last time you truly felt like a child—when your sense of wonder was high and your laughter a resonant ringing of hope. Just like Lucy was a gift to me in a season of pressure, where is the Father opening a door of joy and delight for you? Ask the Father to open your eyes to see His gifts of joy to you in this season of life. Journal His response.

MY YOUNG QUEEN

BY JD GRAVITT
PHOTO BY MORGAN CAMPBELL

Eyes wide open and one month early,
She came into the world full of appetite.
Her hunger made space before her.
Not even six pounds,
She carried the weight of heaven in her tiny heart.
What wealth of snuggles and giggles is traded
For the cost of sleep and the sacrifice of time?
There is no bargaining when it comes to laying down your life.
I do not ask for sleepless nights or welcome the unreasonable crying.

But I would not trade them for her trust in me.
The smile, her smiles, land with great
reward on my heart.
Her curiosity and her constantly expanding world
are mine to steward and cultivate.
Her eyes reveal her thoughts moving around
the landscape of desire.
Strength increases every day,
Her little spirit stands in the love I give
Heal my heart with her tiny voice,
My hands hold all the convenience I stand to lose
And my eyes realize the reward of dependency.
All my battles become her victories,
I no longer face the world only for me,
My life becomes the world for my young queen.

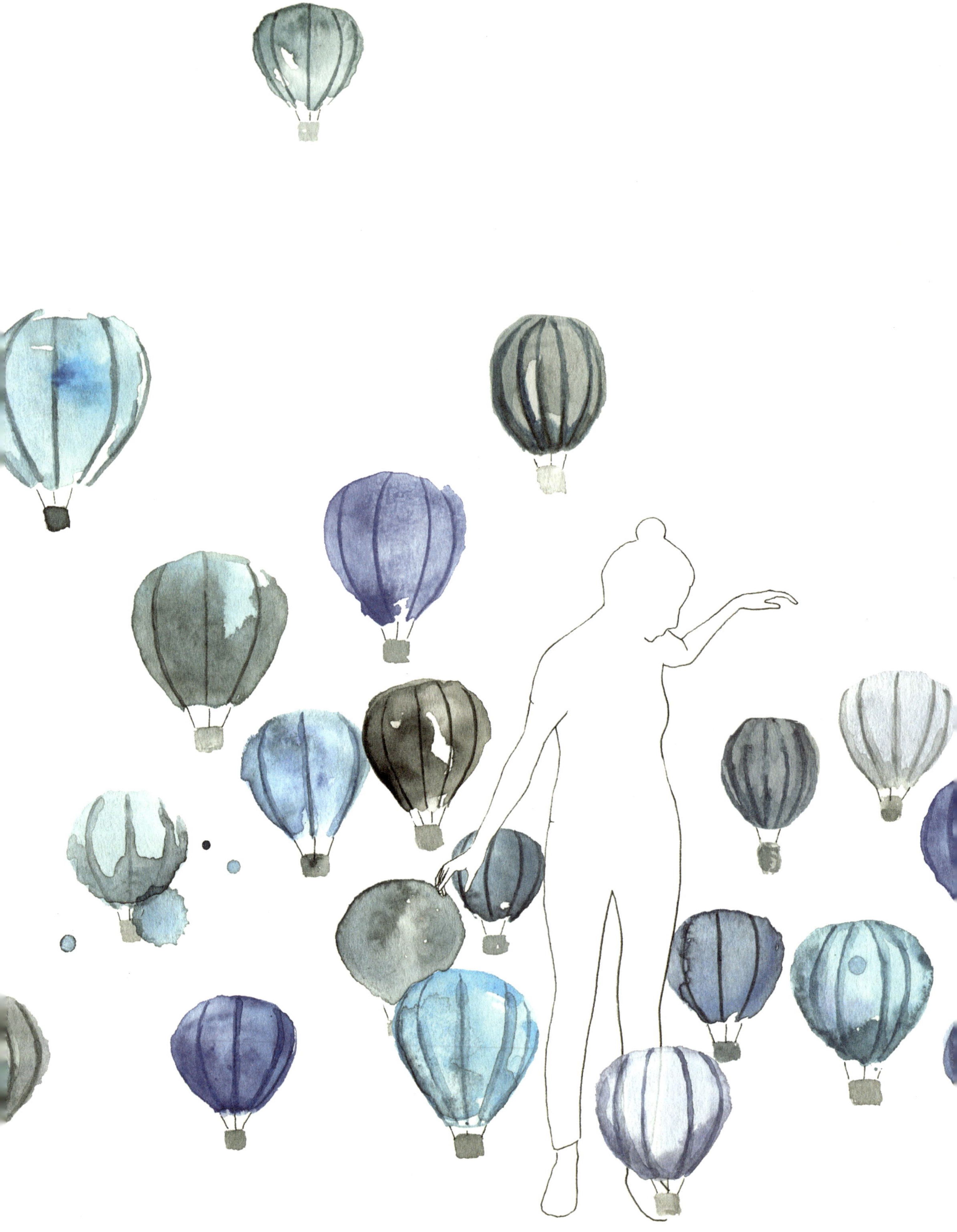

Prayer

PROMPT AND PAINTING BY JUSTINA STEVENS

One day while I was sitting quietly before the Lord, I saw a picture of dozens of small hot-air balloons slowly ascending all around me. I heard the Father say, "Justina, these hot-air balloons are a picture of every moment you've waited on me to fill your heart with a prayer. When your words hit the air and come into unity with what I am doing, they take flight and fill my ears."

He desires hearts that are willing to wait on Him. Today, sit and ask the Father to fill your heart with a prayer. Take your time and don't be afraid of the silence. Learning to wait on God is one of our greatest priveleges. As you pray, imagine each word becoming a hot-air balloon ascending to fill the Father's ears.

AFTERMATH

BY BRIGITTE BELL
PHOTO BY PETER MATTIS

Content and quiet I sit
Unsure how I arrived here
Pondering why I have not moved
Questioning the stillness

The aftermath of bravery
It was not easy
Yet I am here
Still
Settled
Strong

Emotions at a calm
Are they alive?
They are alive
Why so quiet?

Different, not less alive
Resting, Recovering, still

Promise on the horizon
Trust unshaken
Confidence undiminished

Perhaps more ready than I understood
Perhaps stronger than I'd thought possible

Covered in the risk
Covered in the choice
Covered now
Covered always

Good awaits me
Good hunts me down
Good finds

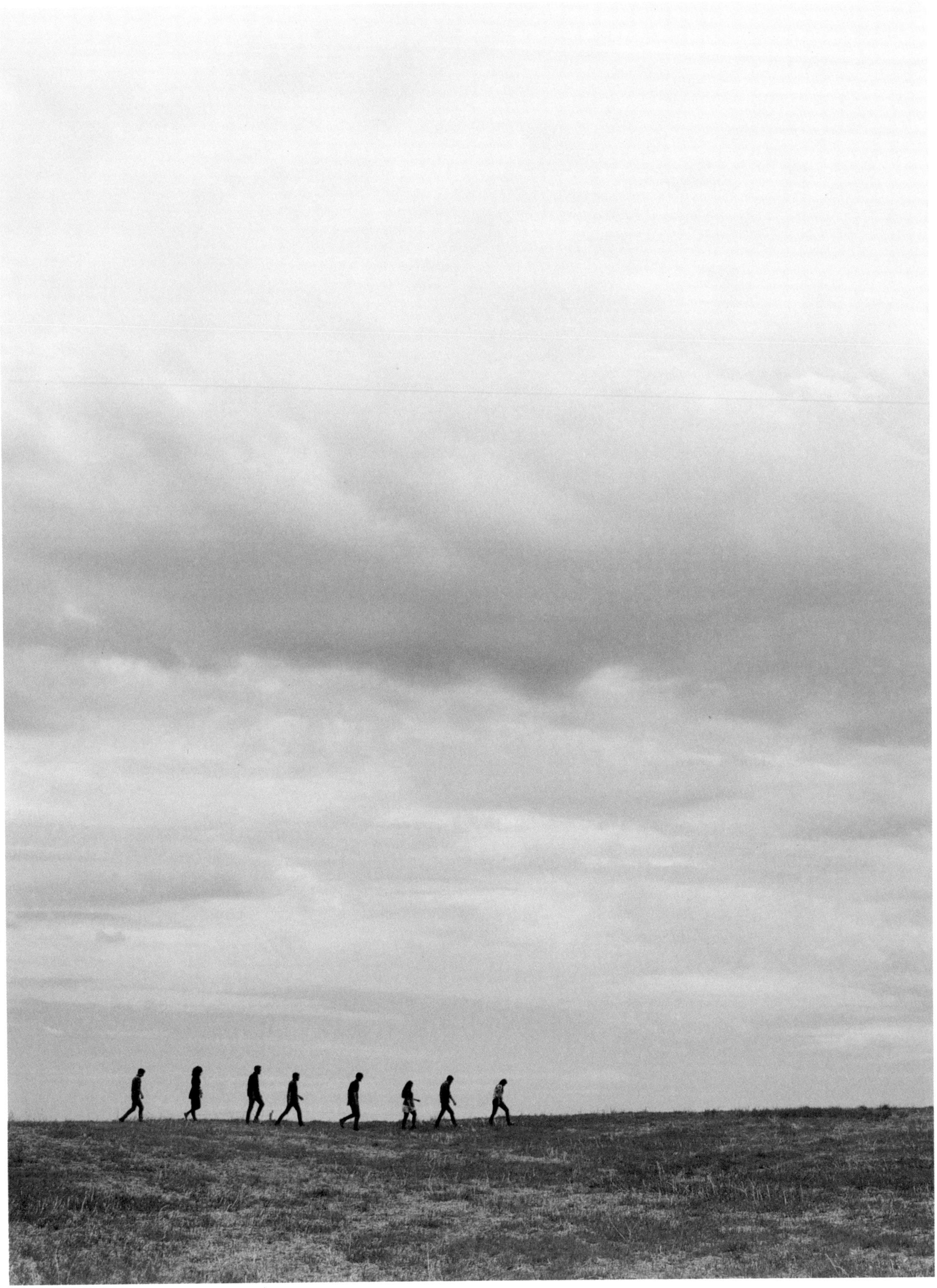

about

THE CAGELESS BIRDS

"We escaped like a bird from a hunter's trap. The trap is broken, and we are free!" Psalm 124:7, NLT

The Cageless Birds is a community of leaders and artisans from Sophia, North Carolina founded by Jonathan and Melissa Helser. We are drawn together by an authentic passion for the gospel of Jesus and a commitment to live out wholeness in community. We believe in the risk of saying yes to flying out of the cage of fear and soaring on the wings of true identity. We have fallen in love with the rhythm of pouring out our lives in ministry and then refilling our hearts in rhythms of family, friendship and creativity. This is sustainability. This is what it means to fly high and build home.

As leaders, we believe in and are committed to seeing a generation transformed by the Gospel. This commitment is walked out through our discipleship school, The 18 Inch Journey. Here, we set a table for students from around the world to come and encounter the love of the Father, the power of the Cross, the sustainability of the Holy Spirit, and the beautiful transformation that happens in community.

As artisans, we come alive in creating goods throughout the year that help support our growing families and the mission of our schools. Whether it's creating music, writing books or cultivating one of our many other art forms, we are anchored with joy in the pursuit of excellence in all that we do.

For more on the Cageless Birds, visit our website and online store at *cagelessbirds.com*.

CONNECT & SUPPORT

VISIT OUR STORE
cagelessbirds.com
TO PURCHASE COPIES, HANDCRAFTED GOODS
& TO READ OUR BLOG

INSTAGRAM
@cagelessbirds

DISCIPLESHIP SCHOOL
18inchjourney.com

WHOLESALE & QUESTIONS
cagelessbirdsstore@gmail.com

EDITOR IN CHIEF
Melissa Helser

CREATIVE DIRECTOR
Justina Stevens

GRAPHIC DESIGNER
Lindsay Vance

COPY EDITORS
Sarah Roach, Justina Stevens, Allie Sampson,
Erin Gravitt and Phyllis Unkefer

Cover photo by Melissa Helser

Handlettered titles and type by Lindsay Vance and Justina Stevens

Blue Heron paintings and washes by Justina Stevens

Nature and Motives photo by Ginny Corbett

Earth Looks Like Family photo by Sydnee Mela

[1] *Cultivate definition: "cultivate." Merriam-Webster.com. Merriam-Webster, 2016.*
[2] *Foundation definition: "foundation." Google.com. Google, 2016.*
[3] *Ascend definition: "ascend." Google.com. Google, 2016.*
[4] *Soar definition: "soaring." Google.com. Google, 2016.*
[5] *Landing definition: "landing." Google.com. Google, 2016.*

All rights reserved.
No portion of this book may be reproduced
without permission from the Cageless Birds.